D1622494

Secrets To Foreclosure Fortunes

By

Cleo Katz

Published by HG Publishing, LLC

Published by: HG Publishing, LLC

PRINTED IN THE UNITED STATES OF AMERICA FOR WORLDWIDE DISTRIBUTION.

© 2008 Cleo Katz, LLC

ISBN 978-1-934959-00-8

Acknowledgments

To my family, my biggest success in life.

*To Family Products who chose me to be
the Foreclosure Messenger nationwide.*

*To Shira Bush for her extraordinary efforts
and attention to detail, and without whom
this book would not have been what it is.*

*Special thanks to Randy Caruso, Producer and
Director of the "Secrets to Foreclosure Fortunes"
infomercial for his creative input and tireless effort.*

*To Linda Gravani for her friendship and
research help in writing this book.*

Table Of Contents

Introduction

*"The teacher is one who
makes two ideas grow
where only one grew before."*

—*Elbert Hubbard*

Hi, and thank you for buying my book "Secrets to Foreclosure Fortunes." I've been buying and selling foreclosure property and conducting seminars for over 29 years.

In the early days of this century, before talking pictures were invented, Hollywood regaled moviegoers with melodramas. The plots of these tear-jerkers were all basically the same — a poor but honest widow is threatened with foreclosure by the evil banker holding the mortgage *(boo, hiss)*. If she doesn't make the required payments by sundown, he will turn her and her beautiful daughter out on the street unless, of course, the girl agrees to marry him *(oh, no!)*.

Just as this innocent young thing is about to give in to the villain's diabolical demands, the handsome hero dashes in with the needed money, pays off the mortgage, and claims the girl for himself *(hooray!)*.

Although times have changed quite a bit since those innocent days, foreclosures are still very much with us. And believe it or not, you can be the hero in one of these real life melodramas. You don't have to be handsome and dashing all you need is some time, good negotiating skills, and the desire to turn a neat profit while helping some homeowners in the process.

This is really a winning situation for everyone. The homeowner walks away with their credit intact and some money in their pocket, the lender gets the mortgage paid up, and the investors earn a good profit.

When I first started I had no money and no experience. I was a divorced mother with two young children to support. I was working in a job as a secretary for a real estate broker who was taking advantage of people in foreclosure. Some of the stories were heartbreaking to me. This man had no conscience. I said to myself there has got to be a better way to deal with this foreclosure problem. I got a list of property in foreclosure and I started knocking on doors and talking to the owners who were in foreclosure to find a solution to their problem.

I will never forget my first foreclosure deal. It was a Saturday morning and I knocked on the door of an elderly lady in her bathrobe. They were about to lose their home at a Trustee's Sale in just three weeks.

I spoke to her and she started to cry. Her husband had suffered a heart attack, lost his job and now they were about to lose their home. They had no money and no place to go.

Twenty nine years ago, I borrowed a little money from a friend and told him I would split the profits with him. Then, I put together a solution for these people. After helping the homeowner, I made a profit of $30,000 that I split that with my friend who had loaned me the money. As a point of information, $15,000 was more money than I had made in an entire year at my job as a secretary. I knew I would do this for the rest of my life, and I also knew I was onto something big!

I personally took ownership of the home after doing a title search on the property with a title company. I found there were three loans on the property. The first loan was foreclosing, which then opened up an opportunity for me to discount the other two loans. If the opening bid at the sale didn't go beyond the first loan, then the second and third loans would get wiped out. I call this "Hidden Equity." I did some fixing up and sold the house three weeks after I took title, making a nice profit.

Through the profits of the sale, I saved the homeowner's credit. I paid for their move to an apartment and gave them money to pay for six month's rent. I remember sitting on the floor with the woman and helping her pack her dishes. I believe I helped restore their self-esteem. You have to realize that lenders are not in the real estate business; they are in the lending business, so I was also able to help the lenders.

This is a working handbook to make money. There is no magic involved. The most important thing is to make up your mind to do something about this foreclosure situation during this unique point in history. You don't need credit or lots of money to take over a real estate loan. That is one of the many secrets I reveal in this book.

You can help the troubled owner save their credit rating and share in the profits. It is important for them to recover and resume their regular economic life, so it becomes a winning situation for everyone.

Now is the greatest opportunity to make money in the foreclosure market. It is like nothing I have ever seen before!

The nationwide crisis since the early 1990's has now led to the highest home foreclosure rate since the Great Depression of the 1930s. The investor who helps out a troubled homeowner is doing everyone a favor.

The three year Adjustable Rate Mortgages, the Liar (or Stated Income) loans and the Sub-Prime loans that people used to get into a home, with no money down and interest only payments, are now driving many Americans into a foreclosure situation.

Right now with homeowners' Adjustable Rate Mortgages (ARMs) coming due, or facing the end of their first three years of their Adjustable Rate Mortgages, their mortgage payments are doubling and people just cannot afford the new higher payments.

Notices of Default, or Pre-Foreclosures, are driving the real estate market down because people with adjustable rate mortgages cannot refinance. Their house is not worth what they paid for it and they are ending up in a foreclosure situation.

Surprisingly, buying and selling foreclosure property requires relatively little start-up capital and can be done on a part-time basis or as an adjunct to your regular job. That's how I started. I didn't have the capital to back myself, so I found an investor and worked on the weekends. It wasn't long before I had made enough money to quit my job and go into the foreclosure business full time.

How much money will you need? That depends on a number of factors, including how far in default the homeowner is, the number of encumbrances against the property, and the physical state of the property. You don't need credit or lots of money to take over a real estate loan. That is one of the many secrets I reveal in this book.

If the property is in the beginning stages of default, it may only require a couple of thousand dollars. However, if the homeowner was already many months behind his payments when the lender started foreclosure proceedings, your cost to fund can be considerably higher.

At the very least, you must be able to cover all the delinquent payments and late charges. This stops the foreclosure process and keeps the banks at bay. Then the liens must be cleared. However, this can be discounted for pennies on the dollar. If the holder of the lien does nothing to protect their investment, they get the same as the homeowner – nothing!

As the final step of the process, the house must be readied for market. That may require no more than a cleaning and a new coat of paint, or it may involve more extensive repairs. If it is so far in arrears that no suitable agreement can be negotiated with the lender, you can always pass it up for something more suitable.

There are plenty of potential backers who would welcome a working partner. They are actively seeking enthusiastic partners who will do all the necessary legwork. When the property is sold, both partners share the profits.

There are a number of ways to find such backers. Friends or relatives are one source (remember, this is not a loan; they will be earning a handsome return). Another alternative is to advertise in the local newspaper or business journal.

Though most people involved in the foreclosure business are interested in single-family homes, all types of property can be acquired this way. The range is tremendous. Some people deal exclusively in commercial and industrial properties or multi-unit buildings and empty lots that they find in the default listings.

This raises the possibility of buying foreclosure property for purposes other than a quick sale. Many of my students are primarily interested in finding new homes while others want income property. It all depends on the portfolio you want to build and the specifics of the deal you develop. This is very much a numbers game. If you understand how to work them you can be very successful, whichever path you take.

Sincerely,

Cleo Katz

The Foreclosure Process

*"Don't find fault.
Find a remedy."*

—Henry Ford

Single Family Homes

Statistics have shown that a financially troubled homeowner who is behind in his mortgage payments and who owes to the lender the extra charges for late payments, foreclosure fees, legal fees and other expenses, will not only end up losing his home, but will probably lose his good credit rating as well. Here is where the "Specialist in Troubled Properties" can step in and help the homeowner!

Single family homes today are the surest and the fastest way to make money in real estate. Forty, fifty, and even a hundred thousand dollars can be earned by investing in single family homes. The profit is not realized until the property is sold, but the profit is there and does accumulate for the owner.

A private party is better able to help the troubled owners and help himself than are the experts. He knows the problems of the consumer. He can take the time and make the effort to work on one deal at a time whether for a required individual home or a part-time business.

Condominium Considerations

A large part of the foreclosure market is in condominiums. There are opportunities to buy condos at distressed prices. Look carefully at the situation before buying, especially at resale opportunities.

The biggest difference between living in a single-family, detached home is you have a buffer of lawn and maybe a fence between you and your neighbors. In a condo, this division is often no more than a common wall. In addition, once you are outside your unit, you are sharing space with the other residents. One of the most important considerations in buying a condo is deciding whether this type of living arrangement is suitable for you and your family.

Cost: Multi-family housing uses less land and is often more economical to build because of common structural components and other design features. Therefore, these units are generally less expensive than detached homes of similar size and quality. (Of course, condos can be very expensive housing when placed in exclusive locations.) Lower priced units are good starters cause of the insulating effect of neighboring units.

Location: Because they take up less land per unit, condos can be developed on high-cost land within major cities. This appeals to people who like being closer to downtown business and entertainment centers. On the other hand, these locations may not be as residential in character as single-family neighborhoods. This is a judgment you must make based on your desired lifestyle.

Low Maintenance: A big attraction for some condo residents is the freedom from many of the routine household tasks. Things like lawn maintenance and outside repairs are generally the responsibility of the association. You pay for these services through your monthly fee, but this is often cheaper than contracting independently for these services.

Lifestyle: Some complexes are specifically designed to promote certain lifestyles. There may be organized social functions for young single adults. Older single people may like the security of having neighbors close by. Elaborate common area facilities may be conducive to entertaining.

Privacy: This is probably the biggest objection many people have to condos. Good design can minimize this problem. Soundproofing in common walls and ceilings, private entryways (often associated with townhouse designs), and private patios and decks can reduce the intrusion of your neighbors.

Control: Much of what you do in your home is determined by the by-laws of the condo and majority rule of the owners association.

Status: In many parts of the United States, condos are indistinguishable from rental apartments. Therefore, you may find that much of the status advantage normally attached to homeownership is lost when you own a condo. In some areas, mortgage financing for these units has been a problem. Lenders are either unfamiliar with condo ownership or feel that the units are not as marketable as and therefore less valuable collateral than, detached homes.

Foreclosure Process

The foreclosure procedure is basically a simple process. Even properties that appear to be over encumbered with debt, can become opportunities.

After several months of non-payment by the owner, the beneficiary (lenders) instructs their trustees to file a Notice of Default and Election to Sell. This notice is recorded at the County Recorders office in the County where the property is located. This recording starts the clock ticking away on the reinstatement period before it goes to public auction.

The property owner has a default period to either reinstate the loan or sell the property.

Some owners choose to sell during this period. This is a wonderful opportunity for you to step in and provide foreclosure solutions for the owner. You can make a lot of money creating a win, win, win situation for everyone. Never take unconscionable advantage of someone in a distressed situation because what goes around comes around! If the default time has elapsed without any action by the owners, the lender now schedules the property for auction.

These owners are in total control of the property up until the auction. Many profitable deals have been made with these motivated owners during these final desperate days.

If the owner does not reinstate or sell the property by the sale date, then the foreclosure auction will take place. The owner is the last person on the totem pole to receive any money. In almost every foreclosure auction the owner loses everything. It is in the best interest of the owner to sell the property to you before the auction.

If no one bids at the foreclosure auction, the lender (the beneficiary who is foreclosing) becomes the owner. The property now becomes a REO (Real Estate Owned).

Buying REO

Lenders are now getting large amounts of properties back due to the avalanche of foreclosures nationwide.

Foreclosures are up 800%. This avalanche of foreclosures is happening because of irresponsible loans created by banks and mortgage lenders to create more business.

If a property has gone back to the foreclosing beneficiary (lenders) contact the lender before he turns the property over to a Real Estate Agent for resale. Refer to the REO section in the back on how to make an offer to a lender.

Trust Deeds

Trust Deeds are used almost exclusively in some states rather than the more common Mortgage Form.

There are three parties on a Trust Deed:

1. TRUSTOR: Owner/Borrower

2. TRUSTEE: Intermediate party who holds title to the property for the protection of the borrower and the lender. (He acts as a "fiduciary" or one in a position of trust –– hence the term "Trust Deed")

3. BENEFICIARY (BENE): The lender who holds the promissory note.

There are two instruments involved in the transaction of a Trust Deed.

The Trust Note is a promissory note which acts as actual evidence of debt and the Deed of Trust which acts as security for the debt.

If the TRUSTOR defaults (is late) with payment(s) of the trust deed note, a foreclosure suit (in court) is not required to collect the loan. The property can legally be sold by the TRUSTEE at public auction at the request of the BENEFICIARY.

If the default is not cured (the loan reinstated) — payments brought current, during the reinstatement period, then all that remains to be done before a public auction is held against the property is that the *date, time* and *place* of the action (called a Trustee's Sale) *be published once each week for three consecutive weeks* in a newspaper of general circulation (check security instrument for your state). Trust Deeds or the Mortgage Form are the security instruments used.

The above example relates to a non-judicial foreclosure which applies to a trustee state (time allowed may differ from state to state.)

A judicial foreclosure is settled through the courts and may take as long as a year. However, the technique and concepts written in this book can be applied in any state. Check the "State Foreclosure Information Sheet" (in the appendix) for the time allowed in your state.

You can get started by looking for all of the foreclosures in your county, and if you are working a mortgage state, make sure you check out the foreclosure laws for your state.

The Foreclosure Process
(Trustee State)

Foreclosure is the process used to enforce a creditor's rights to collect the past-due monies for a debt secured by real estate.

- BENEFICIARY chooses TRUSTEE

- TRUSTEE notified of default in writing by the BENEFICIARY

- TRUSTEE verifies amount due

- TRUSTEE prepares necessary documents

- TRUSTEE records Notice of Default in county where the property is located

- TRUSTEE notifies anyone who has a recorded interest in the property

3-MONTHS + 16 Days REINSTATEMENT PERIOD	5 DAYS BEFORE TRUSTEE SALE FORECLOSURE PERIOD
Notice of Default is recorded, published in local newspaper (one time only).	Notice is posted on property and Notice of Trustee Sale is recorded and published in paper (3 consecutive weeks).
During the Default Period the owner can reinstate back payments, pay off lender in full or deed property to lender (if lender is willing).	During the last 5 day period, the entire loan becomes due.
	If the loan is paid off, then a Full Reconveyance is recorded.
If the loan is reinstated then a Rescission is recorded.	

A public auction (Trustee Sale) is held after the 5-day period, if the loan has note been cured (brought current). The highest bidder receives a Trustee Deed, recorded.

Because it would be impossible to walk you through fifty state examples, the above example relates to a foreclosure in a trustee state. Sharing in the profits with a home owner can be applied in any state.

The Foreclosure

The trustee records a Notice of Default and mails a copy to the trustor. After a period of 3 months and 16 days, a notice of sale must be posted on the property and published in a newspaper at least once a week for 3 weeks. The sale is conducted by the trustee, about 21 days after notice of date.

The proceeds are used to pay the trustee's fees first, then the lien holder's, with the surplus (if any), are given to the trustor.

When property is sold under a trust deed sale, the deed issued by the trustee is known as a *Trustee Deed*.

The following pages will show you how to acquire the property before the trustee's sales, thus eliminating any competition that accompanies a sale.

In some states the Deed of Trust (Trust Deed, TD) is not allowed. They must use the mortgage (to secure their real estate loans) which must be foreclosed judicially –– through the Court system.

Trustee Fees

During the first 3 months and 16 days that a homeowner is in default, he or she can become current by making up all the back payments, late charges and trustee fees.

In the last 5 days (foreclosure period) the homeowner can be required to pay off the entire loan to keep the house.

Reinstating Loans

In some of the transactions, you will make up the delinquent payments during the 3 months and 16 days reinstatement period and you will file a *Rescission* that cancels the foreclosure proceedings.

If you purchase a property during the last 5 days (foreclosure period) you may have to pay the entire loan (always ask the lender if you can reinstate). If the entire loan must be paid, make sure a Full Reconveyance is recorded at the county recorder's office; this removes the cloud from the title and the property can then be sold.

Foreclosure Background

A. Foreclosure — 2 types

    1. Judicial; Court Foreclosure (can take up to a year)

B. California Civil Code (check your state)

    1. Non-judicial; speedy process

        a. 3 months + 16 days: Reinstatement Period

        b. 5 days: Foreclosure Period; entire loan balance becomes due and payable

        c. Trustee's Sale; public auction

C. Opportunities

    1. Pre Default: before default notice is filed; look for ads in your local papers under "For Sale by Owner".

    2. First of Default Period; less cash required out of your pocket. This is a numbers game; this is a harder area to work, but less dollars required.

    3. 20 days before the 5-day Foreclosure Period begins; good pressure period because if the foreclosure enters into the last 5 days, the whole loan becomes due and payable.

    4. Foreclosure Period: the last 5 days; homeowner cannot pay off entire loan; always ask BENEFICIARY for reinstatement.

    5. Trustee's Sale; cash is required.

    6. REO: Real Estate Owned; working with lenders, after they have taken the property back.

    7. Buyer's Broker: a broker that works for you, not the seller.

Foreclosure Process

A. Sequence of Events

1. Property Ownership; determined by the names that appear(s) on the Grant Deed.

2. Situation Change; loss of job; divorce; illness; death; payment due.

3. Payment Missed; time before Notice of Default is filed varies; 2 to 3 months for larger lenders; 1month for private lenders; 4 to 6 months for V.A.; 6 months to 1 year for FHA.

4. Notice of Default and Election to Sell; the BENEFICIARY controls the sale; they can foreclose if the TRUSTOR is one day late.

5. Foreclosure Period; final 5 days before Trustee Sale; the loan is all due and payable.

6. Last Day; Trustee's Sale; the BENEFICIARY can postpone the sale.

B. Players Identified

1. TRUSTOR: Homeowner

2. BENEFICIARY: Lender

3. TRUSTEE: Third party. (usually a title company or an attorney)

C. Information Sources

1. Master Source: County Recorder's Office in the county where the property is located.

2. Sources:

    a. Title Company

    b. Homeowner

    c. Foreclosure Research Service

D. Default vs. Foreclosure

>   1. Default Period: Reinstate Period; 3months and 16 days from Notice of Default. (California)
>
>   2. Foreclosure Period: entire loan becomes due and payable, last 5 days before Trustee's Sale.

E. Action Plan

>   1. Read the daily "Hot Sheets"
>
>   2. Select your properties by location
>
>   3. Look up the properties in Thomas Bros. Guide
>
>   4. Work with letters, send out Cds (Information under Locating Property Owner.), door knocking, Trustee Sales, REOs; or work with a Buyer's Broker.

F. Timing

>   1. 3 weeks after the Notice of Default is filed is a good time to contact the homeowner for the first time.

Dealing With People

Overcome fear by letting the homeowner know about your ethics in the business. Let the homeowner know they're not in foreclosure, the property is. Homeowner benefits by saving their credit moving in an orderly manner, getting cash in their pocket, possible tax benefits and restoring their self-esteem.

>   **F** – Fear
>
>   **E** – Embarrassment
>
>   **A** – Adjust the homeowner's concept of the foreclosure laws and your ethics in the business
>
>   **R** – Right way of purchasing foreclosures

Abandoned Property

1. Inquire among several neighbors. Someone probably knows where the homeowner moved to and they may tell you where, if you can convince them you're not a bill-collector but instead, want to give their former neighbors some money.

2. Or, they may have used a moving van and some neighbor may remember the name on the van, and you can inquire with the moving company for new address.

3. Or, someone will know where he last worked and you can find if anyone there at his former place of employment knows his whereabouts. If he is a union member, his location can be found that way or, at the very least, the union will deliver a letter to him for you through their union channels.

4. If they were in a great deal of financial trouble, and they probably were, they might have had a lawyer. You can check the County Clerk's office for lawsuits against them and, from those records, get the name of his lawyer. Often, a title company can be of assistance in the search for this, too. His lawyer probably will not give you their address, but will get a letter from you to them.

5. Also his neighbors will probably know the names of their relatives and can tell you that.

Returned Mail

There are several "Postal Endorsements" that can be stamped on letters returned to us. The overall endorsement is called "Undeliverable as Addressed" or "Return to Sender". This endorsement breaks down into specific categories which are sometimes also included on the rubber stamp used by the post office. They include the following:

1. "Moved, Left No Address": this means they left and didn't leave any change-of-address card.

2. "No Such Number": this means the envelope is incorrectly addressed. Check phone information (dial 411).

3. "Move, Not Forwardable": this means the same as #1.

4. Check on the internet at www. whitepages.com

5. "Addressee Unknown": this means there's no one at that address by that name. The house could already be sold; or it could be that new people or old renters are living there, but not the owners. The property could also be vacant. Check with phone information and go from there.

With a bit of extra assistance from the postal carrier, there will be a mark in the "Check if no occupant" box on the envelope, telling us that the homeowner has split and left the house.

If the mail is returned with a postal endorsement of "Undeliverable as Addressed" AND it also has an address correction tape (usually yellow or white) on it, the homeowners have moved and the property is either vacant or sold. In such cases, as well as #2 above, a new letter is sent to the current address of the homeowner. The potentially vacant property is, of course, also checked out visually.

When calling phone information, you need to ask for both the phone number and the address. They won't give the address only. Be sure to check the full address with the information operator, i.e, street spelling, city, etc.

If nothing of any consequence results from the above efforts to locate the correct address, you can always contact the trustee to get the correct address.

Exceptions To Illegal
Home Remodeling To The Buyer

Many existing homes in Southern California contain added rooms or some type of remodeling for which no permit was obtained. When a homeowner wishes to work on his property, he is required to obtain a building permit. The purpose of the permit is to ensure that the owner or his contractor complies with local building and zoning codes. Some property owners do not obtain a permit out of ignorance, or perhaps they want to avoid a property tax increase. Additions made without a permit can be bad news for the seller and can delay the closing of escrow for the buyer.

It is technically against the law to sell a home that contains an illegal add-on. In any case, the seller must disclose this to the buyer as well as to the broker. In some cases, the add-ons were so well done that they are almost invisible to the eye. Only an expert would be aware of the fact that any additional construction had been done. In the case of an add-on that was done according to code, it is generally a simple matter to obtain a building permit and call for an inspection. In some cases, the building inspector could require that a section of wall be removed to show that it was framed properly and that the electrical wiring was enclosed in conduit, etc. When the add-on is not constructed according to code, anything could be needed, from minor reconstruction to total tear-down of the add-on.

When the add-on is in violation of zoning regulations, there are two alternatives. One is total demolition of the add-on and restoration of the house to its original size. An alternative would be to obtain a zoning variance. Common examples include encroachments into side yards, rear yards, or the addition of a second dwelling unit of a lot zoned for single family use.

ALWAYS ASK the seller of the property that you are buying if there are any known building or zoning code violations on the property. Include a statement to this effect in your offer to purchase and have it signed by the seller.

Searching A Title

STEP 1. ASSESSOR'S OFFICE

Locate the property by street address or the owner's name. There will be a record, generally a card, showing the following:

a. When the property was purchased

b. Purchase price

c. Tax Assessor's land and improvements value

d. Deed Book and Page number where the deed is recorded

The tax assessor's offices are the least standardized of all courthouses functions. Therefore, records will vary widely from office to office. Familiarize yourself with the office in your area. If you have any questions, ask. The clerks will be more than willing to help you.

STEP 2. LOCATING THE DEED

The Deed Room will generally be located in the vicinity of the Circuit Court. If the Deed Book and Page Number was available at the Assessor's Office, locate the proper volume of the Deed Book, turn to that page, and you'll have it. If you have only the date of purchase, locate the Grantee's Book for the year, find the transaction under the owner's name, and it will indicate the Deed Book and Page Number.

In several states, the Grantor-Grantee Index is supplemented or replaced by a Tract Index in which all recorded deeds and liens are indexed by the property rather than by the owner's name.

From the deed, you will find the following:

1. Names of owners (exactly as the deed MUST be transferred)

2. Legal description of the property

3. Map Book and Page Number of the physical plant map

4. Grantor's source of the property, and Deed Book and Page number of THAT document

STEP. 3 LOCATING A MORTGAGE OR TRUST DEED

Most mortgages and trust deeds are taken out at the time that title is transferred. Therefore, look at the year pages immediately following the deed. Failing this quick method, locate the Grantor's Book for that year and locate the owner's name. The Deed Book and Page will soon be shown there. Armed with this information, go back to the Deed Room and look up the mortgage/ trust deed instrument. You will want to know this information:

1. Loan type (VA, FHA, Conventional)

2. Original amount of the loan

3. Date the first payment was due

4. Date the last payment was due

5. Interest rate

6. Payoff and assumption information

7. Beneficiary

8. Legal description of the property

9. Foreclosure information

10. Prior liens, if any

11. Release of lien

Copies of all documents can be obtained for a small fee.

STEP 4. FINDING OTHER LIENS

Go back to the Grantor's Book. Beginning with the original mortgage entry, carefully check every entry from the point to the present date, looking for any liens affecting the property. Make a note of the Deed Book and Page of each lien. When finished, return to the Deed Room and check each one.

STEP 5. JUDGEMENTS

The last step is to locate the Defendant's Judgment Index and look for the owner (and spouse) from the date of the mortgage to the present. Anything you may find will reference a Judgment Book and Page which, when found, will give you the following:

a. Person owed

b. Amount owned

c. Date of Judgment

d. Date satisfied (if paid)

It is important to remember that a judgment constitutes a lien on the property. A judgment lien can foreclose, but only subject to mortgages and superior liens. The judgment is a lien against ALL of the real property owned by the debtor at the time the judgment is entered.

Title Company

The Customer Service department of a good title company can provide you with the same information available from the recorder's office. However, they will not do all the research for you on every property. Use them sparingly.

Junior Lienholders

Junior lienholders, if any, can be discovered in the following manner:

1. From the Notice of Default, note the date and recording data on the foreclosing lien.

2. Determine the name of the present property owner and the date he purchased the property.

3. At the County Recorder's Office, check under the original debtor's name, starting with the date the foreclosing lien was originated and continuing up until the date the property was sold (if it was solD or the present date (if the original owner still owns the property). Look for other deeds of trust recorded against the property. These will be junior to the foreclosing lien.

4. Look backward in time to determine when the debtor acquired the property and if the foreclosing lien is the first trust deed or if there are other liens ahead of it. If there are one of more liens senior to the foreclosing lien, determine the present amount owing on the senior liens.

5. If the property had been sold by the original debtor, check under the new owner's name for any other deeds of trust recorded against the property from the time of purchase to the present date.

6. If the owner, or debtor, owns more than one property, you will have to look at each deed of trust to determine if it applies to the subject property.

Buying The Property Before The Auction

*"Many of life's failures
are people who did not
realize how close they were
to success when they gave up"*

—Thomas Edison

Buying The Property Before The Trustee Sale

Once you have found a property that looks like a good buy, you have to analyze the numbers to see if it really is a good investment. If a substantial profit can be made after all costs are considered, then the property is a good investment.

The only sensible way to analyze a property is to put down cold hard numbers. Put the pencil to a deal. Use a math formula.

Stick to this format and you will make a good evaluation of the figures:

- Any cost you plan for which does not materialize increases your profit.

- Any cost you don't plan on decreases your profit.

- If the deal doesn't have profit going in, it will not have profit coming out.

Verify Numbers: It is very important for you to make sure that you have up-to date figures to work with before you go to the property and knock on the door.

Holding Costs: Assuming your title search showed no liens or judgments you are prepared to deal with then, let's plan to hold the property for a period of 30 days beyond the average time for market value sales in that neighborhood. This applies only if you plan to sell and not keep the property as a rental.

Down Time: During this holding period you need to consider "down time". That is the time a property is not really at its best to show and sell because the previous owner hasn't moved and the repairs haven't been made.

Cost to Sell: Calculate the closing cost into your acquisition costs. Now let's take a look at sales costs. If you list with a Realtor, you will have to pay commission when your property is sold. Always remember commission is negotiable.

The best times I have found to deal with the owners are as soon as they receive their default notices.

If someone is in foreclosure, one of the things that they generally do is lie to people coming to discuss the situation with them. They all had one recurring theme: "We're not in trouble anymore."

Since they have a problem with their mortgage or security deed, I will sit down with them to see if there is any way we can figure out how to save the house from the sale steps.

While you are talking, watch for reactions in their face and body language. You keep your cool and stay relaxed; and try to relax the owner.

Develop rapport-get in the door: Your whole approach needs to be geared toward getting you into the house. So, at the door, you have about thirty seconds to begin to develop a rapport with these people.

Leave on a friendly basis: If you do not get in, then leave on a friendly basis with a comment such as "I'll check the file again in about a week or ten days, if it still hasn't been settled, I'll see you again, fair enough?"

Getting in the door is crucial to buying the property. There is a way to have the property owner call you for an appointment. No door knocking (audio business card or CD sent)!

See if you can figure out any sensible way to keep the property owner from going to Trustee's Sale.

Show empathy: You are planting the seed for them to sell the house to you rather than to just anyone.

Be professional: When you are seated with the owners, it is best to be friendly but maintain a calm, cool, professional manner.

Ask questions which require a detailed answer: Ask them how they got into foreclosure. Many times they will tell you everything you want to know to make the buy. They will reveal many things if you ask questions which requires a fairly long answer, and a comment like "Oh really?" signals them to tell you more.

Do they have an answer for their problem? Ask them, then listen to their answer.

Stop their procrastination – get them to act: They are in their situation because in many cases, they just wouldn't do something such as put the house up for sale or try to negotiate with the lender. You have to make them want to do something.

Explain what will happen if they go through foreclosure. Their credit will be ruined and if the state permits a deficiency judgment, and the foreclosure sale does not bring enough money to cover the cost of the judgment, they can be driven to bankruptcy.

You will buy the property from them or at the auction. But you plan to go to the sale and bid on the property in case you can't work something out with them.

The most serious part of the foreclosure to them as relates to getting another house is that no mortgage company will lend them any money if they have a foreclosure on their record. So it's important to stop the foreclosure if possible.

A very intelligent negotiating technique is to repeat their objections and say, "Is this the only thing that is keeping you from making positive decisions?" If they say yes, then begin to yes-condition them and destroy their objection by pointing out more benefits of your proposition such as saving their credit, not being embarrassed by their belongings being put on the street, not having to move immediately.

Remember, you are a problem solver. Never take advantage of someone in foreclosure. It could happen to you!

How To Speculate In Distressed Property

1. Don't argue with the homeowner; time is on your side.

2. Do keep in contact. Let the homeowner see that you are interested in his welfare.

3. Don't believe everything the homeowner tells you. They may say the delinquent payments have been brought current. Keep in touch.

4. Do ask questions. Fill out your Cost Breakdown Sheet before making any commitments.

5. Don't be discouraged because a homeowner brings his delinquent payments current. He may have gone out and borrowed the money, or had the first and second Trust Deed holder advance the money. If this is the case, they how have two problems:

    a. Keeping up to date with the current payments and expenses.

    b. Paying back the borrowed money.

6. Do warn the homeowner NOT to sign an "Exclusive Right to Sell" agreement with a Broker, because this will jeopardize their position to deal freely with you (or anyone else), especially as the foreclosure deadline draws near. (Unless you are a Real Estate Agent wanting to get a listing).

7. Do appraise their home out loud. Walk around the house, talking to yourself: "Let's see, would I have to paint it? Wallpaper? Redo the kitchen? Give the pool an acid bath?" etc.

8. Don't address the homeowner directly about repairs that may be needed; this may cause a conflict or an "I say this, you say that" situation. Talk to yourself out loud while you fill out your Repair Sheet.

9. Do not take NO for an answer. If this home is not for sale today, it will be with in a few months; 90% of them are.

10. Don't forget to always leave the door open in ALL your conversations with the homeowner. You always have other homes in the area that you are working on. So, the offer you make today may not be valid tomorrow, should you make a deal elsewhere.

11. Do tell the homeowner that you are working with limited capital and that you can only purchase one home at a time. Time is of the essence for both of you.

12. Do tell the homeowner never forget that if their home goes into foreclosure, their credit rating will be ruined. It will hinder any further purchases on a time payment plan. Also, if the property was

foreclosed as a mortgage in court, they may be subject to a Deficiency Judgment.

COMMENT: In California, most all foreclosures are through Trustee's Sales; therefore, there would be no Deficiency Judgment.

13. Do remind the homeowner that each day they wait they are getting further behind on their payments. They are also accumulating late charges, which can put them into a situation where you or anybody else will have a more difficult time taking over their situation and saving their credit, to say nothing of the property taxes that are also accumulating.

14. Don't just get the husband's signature on the Equity Purchase Form when buying a house; get the wife's signature, too. Get signatures for ALL parties whom you even suspect of having any interest in this property.

15. Do talk softly; never argue with the homeowner.

COMMENT: Keep in mind that you are in the business of buying and selling houses. The effort you make today will be the $$$$$ profit you make tomorrow.

16. Don't deal with the lending institution before you have looked up the home owner. Homeowner first; Lender, second.

17. DO NOT lock up the homeowner with a deposit; it's a California foreclosure law that no monetary exchange or transfer of any interest may take place for 5 days after the signing of the Purchase Contract.

18. Do negotiate with the holder of the Second Trust Deed, regardless of who started the foreclosure action. Here is an excellent opportunity to reap extra profits by getting a discount. If the First Trust Deed goes into foreclosure, the Second Trust Deed holder must make up the back payments to protect their interest. In most cases, you can point out that you are willing to cure the default and remedy the situation ONLY if you can purchase the Second Trust Deed at a discount.

19. Do try to get a large cash down payment as you can when selling the house (this, too is part of your profit). Your selling points to the prospective Buyer are; they are 1) buying for a few thousand dollars LESS than any other comparable house around and 2) saving a Broker's commission. (If you are not using a Real Estate Agent to sell it.)

20. Don't quit working your Default lists. You want another house to go onto when you sell your present one. Keep the ball rolling.

SUMMARY

The most important part of this, or any other business is your Mental Attitude. Your daily thoughts are the motivation instrumentality of your earning capabilities.

All the knowledge, education, and instruction you can possibly obtain without power or substance are useless unless you have a positive "I Know It Can Be Done" approach to your new business.

When you go into a home, always go in with a happy "I want the best for everybody concerned" approach. Yes, they may be in trouble now. But you are providing a very great service: you are saving these people from foreclosure.

The Basic Steps Of Pre-Foreclosure Buying

Let's briefly review the methods by which you can help defaulting home-owners solve their problems and receive a substantial reward for doing so.

You must investigate the seller's problems. When you have found out what he needs, negotiate a purchase of his equity and finally, sign the Equity Purchase Agreement. Remember, all the parties who signed the original deed, the Grant Deed, must sign the Equity Purchase Agreement, unless an original interest has been disposed of.

When a person is in default, he or she receives mail from other foreclosure buyers and from a lender who wants to lend out even more money. Expect the owners to be pursuing several alternatives. If they are not happy with your proposal, they will look until the final hours. Plan on this and keep solving their problems or you may lose your prospective bargain.

Buying before the sale is easier for you if the owner is running out of time. The really motivated sellers will answer your inquires, letters, and house calls about four to six weeks before the Trustee's Sale, when they realize that the foreclosure clock is running down. Think about the problems of the owner at this point: no money, no place to go, and no alternatives.

Be sure the seller understands that you will pay them only when they have left the premises and removed all of their personal possessions. People pay for solutions. The homeowner will need help with moving, garage sales, transferring the utilities, and a great deal of understanding. If you intend to succeed again and again you'll need to establish a position attitude and handle the homeowner's problems.

Possession of the property might require that you evict the former owner. If the owner is not receiving enough money to move and get re-established, I'd suggest you pay for the move and the initial cost of renting an apartment. This cost is insignificant when compared to the time and effort of an eviction. The dollar cost will add up rapidly in the eviction process with the attorney fees, mortgage payments, property taxes, filing fees, insurance, and property damage. If the owner is irrational, you should probably walk away from the deal. The foreclosure marketplace is full of opportunities that make sense.

There is another type of transaction you may be inclined to walk away from, even though the seller is motivated to the point of desperation. What about the seller who contacts you one day before the sale? If you normally purchase property in California and use a Home Equity Purchase Agreement, Section 1965 of the Civil Code requires that you allow the owner a five-day right of rescission. But you don't have five days. The Civil Code in California also allows the home equity purchaser to buy the property just before it goes on the auctioneer's block. For example, even if a property is scheduled to be sold at 10:00 a.m., the law allows you to buy it at 8:00 a.m. Do your homework.

If you purchase before the sale, you must know what you are purchasing. You have very little time to do a thorough title search, but you must find out about the existence of any encumbrances or liens on the property.

Get a postponement and have a Home Equity Purchase Agreement signed and agreed to by all parties. You need the postponement to review the records at the County Recorder's Office. Then you will be knowledgeable enough to purchase the property with its known liens and encumbrances.

Finding A Missing Owner

If the house is vacant, check to see if the electricity was shut off. This will tell you how long the property has been vacant. Check with the neighbors if they left a forwarding address. "You can share in the profits," are six magic words to the homeowner.

When you tell the homeowner they can share in the profits – it is a psychological breakthrough. They are now part of the action.

CALL NOW!

866-472-7406

EXT. 650

CKBIC401

ACHIEVE YOUR DREAMS!

Call To Get Started:

866-472-7406

EXT. 650

If you want to buy the house for yourself, ask them "what is the least amount they will take for the equity in their home." You now have an idea of what they would settle for. Remind them if they go to sale, their credit is ruined and they will receive nothing at the sale.

Remember to talk softly and let them see you have their welfare in mind. Make sure you don't pay the homeowner until you have possession and have inspected the property, and the title is clear of liens and judgments.

When homeowners are still in the house:

1. Use the "Share in the Profits Approach"

2. Fill out the History Sheets

3. Do three comparables

4. Sign Equity Purchase Form (check your state for contracts needed)

5. Open Title Search

6. Have Deed signed over to you and notarized

7. Record Deed (As soon as the Title Search comes back and there are no liens, or clouds on the title). Record the Deed at the County Recorder's Office, make sure they give you the right one back. Do this in person right after the Title Search has come in with no problems.

An added benefit to getting the deed signed over is to let the owners remain in the house until sold (deducting the rent from their share of the profits).

If the house is occupied by a tenant:

1. Locate owners

2. Fill out your History Sheets, etc.

3. Offer owner "to Share in Profits"

4. You can keep tenants and continue to collect rent

5. You can have them move out or let the new buyers decide

Remember, in any transaction never give any money to the party that is living in the house until the moving van is outside and they're out the door and the house has been left as agreed upon.

Do not give any money to the person that has left the house (husband or wife) for their share in the house until Title is clear and you have taken ownership. In a divorce situation, you can have both parties "share in the profits".

Foreclosure Stall

Many times you will notice that a troubled owner who had been going along with everything you are saying suddenly beings to stall. The stall is simply his way of saying that he would like to have more time to consider his decision. He would either like to discuss things with his wife or he would like to consult with somebody else. He isn't ready to make a move. Although the troubled owner usually understands the benefit of your deal and believes it will work, at that moment he lacks the confidence in himself to take immediate action.

The key to overcoming this kind of behavior lies in expressing total personal reassurance to the troubled owner. You can do this in the following manner:

1. Be willing to listen to all his comments. Let him get it all out so that you can understand what he is thinking about.

2. Before reacting to his stall, make some kind of agreeing statement. Tell him that you probably would be thinking the same way if you were in his shoes.

3. Remind the troubled owner that time is of the essence in this particular case.

4. Convert his stalling into a feeling of self-confidence. You can do this by repeating your whole presentation. Go back to the very beginning with your comments about the possibility of you doing some good for him and good for yourself.

5. Reassure him strongly that you know what you are doing and that if he goes along with you he will have the benefits you promised.

6. Ask him if he believes that you will do what you say you can do. If he says yes, then repeat that time is of the essence, and you want to go ahead with this deal as quickly as possible. Tell him you'd like to get

right down to the closing details. If he says no, ask him for specific reasons why and then tackle those reasons.

You should be able to handle all kinds of objections and all kinds of strategy a troubled owner may be using if you are interested in his property. The truth is that you are not going to make any money for yourself unless you help him. So the sooner you deal with any reservations the owner might have, the better for both of you.

The troubled owner needs personal attention. You must remember he has great emotional as well as financial problems. He does not want to be treated indifferently. He wants and needs a one-to-one relationship, so by talking directly to the troubled owner, you increase your chances of success.

You can show understanding of the strains he is undergoing. You have the opportunity to offer real sympathy for his problems. At any rate, time is important. The cards must be put on the table. As quickly as possible, the owner must realize his time is running out. There is only one route to take to save his credit rating and to salvage some kind of money from his property.

He may try to play the game of offer and counter-offer. Remind him that time is working against him. Now is the time to sit down and determine once and for all if something can be worked out. It is very important at all times that he should know what is going on, even though you will analyze the profit potential privately.

Remind the owner that the offer is contingent upon the examination of the other facts and on everything being represented. You have only so much time to work on deals so therefore it is the best interest of both sides to reach an acceptable price.

Beneficiary Statement

Property owners who want to pay off a mortgage and remove a lien against their property, but who are unfamiliar with the procedures involved must do the following: The first step a borrower must take is to request a beneficiary statement from his/her lender, which specifies the amount required to pay off a loan.

A beneficiary statement must be in writing and contain the following:

1. The amount of the unpaid balance and the interest rate on the note secured by the Deed of Trust.

2. The amount of any overdue principal and interest installment payments.

3. The amount of any periodic payments.

4. That date on which the note is due.

5. The most current date to which real estate taxes and special assessments have been paid.

6. The amount, term, and premium of hazard insurance coverage in effect.

7. Any charges, costs, or expenses paid or incurred by the beneficiary which have become a lien on the property.

8. Whether the financing may be transferred to a new borrower (buy subject to).

Under this law, the term "beneficiary" refers to a mortgage (lender) or beneficiary of a mortgage or Deed of Trust, or his/her assignee.

An abbreviated form of beneficiary statement, known as a payoff demand statement, is also available. Prepared by a beneficiary in response to a written request by an entitled person, it must specify in writing the amount required, as of the date of preparation, to fully satisfy the note. The payoff demand statement must also include information necessary to calculate the payoff amount on a per diem basis for 30 days.

Who May Request A Statement?

The beneficiary must provide a state to any "entitled person" who request one. Under the new law, an entitled person is defined as:

1. The borrower or his/her successor in interest.

2. Any beneficiary of a junior Trust Deed.

3. Anyone who holds a junior lien or encumbrance.

4. An escrow agent acting as an escrow holder. (This may include a licensed real estate broker, bank, title company, or attorney at law acting in this capacity.)

Additionally, an agent acting on behalf of an entitled person may request a beneficiary statement with the same effect as if the entitled person had made the request personally.

How And When To Request A Statement

If the mortgage or deed of trust is being paid voluntarily, an entitled person may request a beneficiary statement at any time. The beneficiary, in turn, must send the beneficiary statement of payoff demand statement to the trustor or any other entitled person via the mail within 21 days after the receipt of his/her written request.

If the loan is subject to recorded Notice of Default, however, an entitled person must request a beneficiary statement no later than two months after the Notice of Default is recorded. Furthermore, the beneficiary does not have to prepare and deliver a payoff demand statement unless the borrower's written request is received prior to the first publication of a Notice of Sale.

If the beneficiary has more than one place of business, then the entitled person must make the request at the branch or office address set forth in the payment billing notice of payment book.

Beneficiary Must Honor Information

An entitled person, such as a borrower, can rely upon –– and a beneficiary must honor –– the unpaid balance amount and any other information detailed in a statement. If the amount specified in the statement is paid, then the beneficiary must execute a request for reconveyance to remove the lien.

Foreclosure Support Team

If you promise a title company to bring them your closings, some may give you free "pencil searches". That is, they will allow you to call them with just the addresses of a property, and they will rush a quick check on it to tell you what mortgages, liens, or whatever might be tied to that property so you can make a judgment as to whether to make an offer or not.

When was the last time you took your banker or mortgage lender to lunch? Don't laugh. I've made many deals from personal phone calls from lenders I've taken to lunch. They call to ask if I want to take off their hands properties that have come back to them through foreclosure; or, if I want to buy, at a discount (of course!) a mortgage they are about to foreclose on.

Mortgage bankers normally make first-mortgage loans. Mortgage brokers can also make first mortgage loans; but, make most of their business deals with second or third mortgages. Please realize, the commission to a mortgage lender is not called "commission" on the closing statement; rather their fees are called "points".

Investors

To find out what interest return investors are looking for in your area, call a few mortgage brokers and ask them what is the lowest interest-rate private lenders will agree to lend their money out at. Also, check with local banks and savings institutions to see what rates they are offering on short term and long term CDs. You can always offer better rates because real estate offers so many better advantages to money invested.

Competition

What competition? It is all too common for readers to imagine competition out there. But, the facts show that fear to be unfounded.

You probably know more about foreclosures than most Realtors in your area put together. Some Realtors may purchase distressed properties; but, they do not know how to do it the professional way.

Often, in fact, a Realtor may list for-sale a foreclosure property and never even know—because the owner is too proud to admit to the truth and lists in hopes of a fast sale to solve the financial distress. Also, the owner fears if the truth is aired, the Realtor and/or possible buyers will not offer as high a sale price for his or her home.

Most investors are not working financially distressed property leads because 1) either they do not know all the sources you do, or 2) they don't have the time to do all the research. They will end up buying properties they accidentally stumble on themselves, or are pointed out to them by a Realtor.

The fact of the matter is that most foreclosures revert back to the lenders, who follow by mere default. No one bids on them. Competition? What competition? You have none. The only one standing between you and financial success is yourself. Your time for doing something is NOW.

A loan is considered to be delinquent after the due date has passed with no payment made, and before the lender can legally declare the loan in default.

Of course, this time period varies from state to state and depends on the type of language used in the security instrument.

If you have established good rapport with mortgage companies you may very well learn of these impending foreclosures before they are even filed.

If you do not, and the loan goes into default, the lender, under a judicial foreclosure, will file a notice of lis pendens and complaint which will be recorded in the county courthouse in which the property is located, or whichever county building houses such recordings.

In a power-of-sale foreclosure, depending upon the state, the lender simply publishes a notice in the newspaper that the loan is in default, that he has accelerated the balance due, together with reasonable cost, and advertises the property for a certain number of weeks prior to the sale date.

The number of weeks he must advertise, and the sale date after this advertisement, is set by state law.

In trust deeds states, the trustee files formal notice of default prior to any advertised notice of sale. Power-of-Sale States have the final say by whoever holds the power of sale.

When you discover the impending foreclosure your job is to gather all the information necessary to make judgment as to whether or not you should even go to see the owner about buying the property.

What difference does it make if you have to knock on ten doors before you get your first deal? I knocked on 33 before I got my first.

Don't be surprised, at all, if the net profit on your first deal is in excess of $20,000. Mine took five weeks from start to finish, and netted by partner and myself over $35,000.

Investor's Agreement

An agreement with an investor should spell out the responsibilities and liabilities of all parties involved with the transaction.

It should state how the title in the property is to be conveyed.

It should state who will supply the cash, and when; who will receive the proceeds of the sale, and the amount to be shared; and it should set definite time limits.

Avoid partnership agreements. They increase your liability. A partnership must file a separate tax return.

Do's And Don'ts For Investors

DON'T USE LAND CONTRACTS

Land contracts can be a disaster for both buyer and seller. The buyer may have to file a lawsuit to obtain title if the seller dies, refuses to convey the title, absconds with the money, records additional liens against the property, or cannot be found. Land contracts are also undesirable for the seller because, even if the buyer defaults in the purchase, the buyer may be entitled to a refund of all money paid to the seller throughout the years, less the reasonable rental value during the time the buyer was in possession.

USE AITDs INSTEAD

Instead of using a land contract, use an all-inclusive trust deed (AITD), which will accomplish the same objective as a land contract. The benefits of an AITD are that the buyer obtains immediate title, the seller can often pick up some extra interest on his carryback, the seller cannot mortgage the property after escrow closes, and the seller regains title at a Trustee Sale. (Some newer land contract forms also authorize trustee's sales.)

ALWAYS RECORD THE DEED

Occasionally, a buyer and seller will agree not to record the grant deed until a much later time, so that the County will not be alerted to a Proposition 13 reassessment. This nonrecordation can be devastating to the buyer. Without recordation, a buyer cannot obtain title insurance, the seller can convey the property to someone else, the seller can mortgage the property, or the seller may refuse to deliver the deed when later demanded by the buyer. The dollars saved by delaying the Prop 13 reassessment (assuming that the County does not learn of the unrecorded transfer) is miniscule compared with the risks assumed by the buyer if no recordation is accomplished.

DON'T USE "NOMINEE"

Purchase contracts often identify the buyer as "John Doe or nominee". Certain California cases hold that, under some circumstances, the word "nominee" makes the contract illusory and invalid. Instead, use the word "assignee" in the purchase contract to identify the buyer, as follows: "John Doe or assignee".

TITLE POLICIES

Buyers should try to include in their purchase contract a section stating that the seller shall provide an "ALTA" title policy rather than the usual "CLTA" title policy. The CLTA insures against only those documents recorded with the County Recorder. The ALTA policy insures against all the items covered by the CLTA policy, plus additional non-recorded items such as encroachments, discrepancies in boundary lines, and possible rights of tenants in possession. Sellers, on the other hand, since they customarily pay for the policy, should insist on only a CLTA policy or demand that the buyer pay the extra cost for an ALTA policy.

BALLOON PAYMENTS

Civil Code Section 2966 requires that the lender or seller carrying back paper must give the borrower or buyer at least 90 days written notice before a balloon payment is collectible. Failure to give this notice extends the due date to 90 days following the delivery of a tardy notice.

Signing The Grant Deed

First, the Five Day Contract (the cooling off period for the homeowner) should have been signed. After the 5 days have passed (5 business days, Saturday included) and you have checked out the liens, and had preliminary title search done (by the title company), you can then have the Grant Deed signed over you.

It is well to review the summary figures and repeat the reasoning being the offer. By staying with all the fundamentals outlined, nine times out of ten, an agreement will be signed. Make sure the deed is correct. All information on the deed, transferring the property, must be exactly as on the deed the seller received from the Lending Institution.

Time is the important factor. As soon as the deed is signed over by the owner, it must be taken immediately to the county recorder's office to record it. After waiting for it, a copy must be taken right to the title company. The buyer must be sure that his name is first on it and that any liens that come in afterwards will be added after his name and would be invalid.

You should always obtain a certified copy of documents that you are recording since your original won't be mailed back to you from the County Recorder's office for about three weeks.

A Six Day Contract does not have to take place if you are moving in the house yourself.

In other words, "owner occupied," or if the trustor (homeowner) is renting out the house. The interpretation of the law says, "You are not moving the owner out of his residence."

The Six Day Contract does not apply to Commercial or Industrial properties.

You are still going to need a contract (use the Six Day Contract) but modify it. Also, leave enough time to do your title search.

TRANSFER THE TITLE

No real estate transaction is complete until the property changes hands. In order to buy the title and receive the deed on the property it is necessary to fill out correctly and record certain deeds. While the details may vary from state to state, the basic requirements are essentially the same.

RESELL THE NEWLY PURCHASED PROPERTY

In many cases you may elect to resell the acquired property at a profit.

KEEPING AND LEASING THE NEWLY ACQUIRED PROPERTY

In many cases you may elect to keep the new acquisition and lease it out for income.

Ownership Transfers

Make sure the deed is correct. All the information on the deed, transferring the property, must be exactly as on the deed the seller received from the lending institution. If the seller's middle initial is already B as in Barbara, but his deed shows a T as in Tom so that the deed written out is exactly as the grant deed shows.

Too many titles have been messed up because people have made mistakes either copying the information from the bottom of the sheet supplied by the information service, by the newspaper, or from the seller. In no case should anything be used but the original information taken off the grant deed.

Time is the important factor. As soon as the deed is signed over by the owner, you must take it immediately to the recording office to record it. Get a copy, and take it right to the title company. Make sure that your name is first on it and that any liens that come in afterwards will be added after your name and would be invalid.

Ownership transfers are affected in many different ways. You will have to be sure of state and county laws in your own area.

Generally the three most common methods used in most areas are:

1. **Joint Tenancy Grant Deed:** Here both husband and wife are owners of property. Everything is recorded and listed in both names. So any conveyance to you as the new buyer must have the signatures of both owners exactly as they appear on the original conveyance to them.

2. **Individual Grant Deed:** Essentially the same as above, except only one name appears as the owner.

3. **Quit Claim Deed:** This is used when there are special circumstances that prevent a normal grant deed transfer. There may be financing or legal problems. All this does is have the owner convey whatever rights of ownership he has to the buyer. It is really a "buyer beware" situation. Only seasoned investors, with good legal advice, should use this method of acquiring properties.

You will be able to save extra charges associated with real estate transfers by doing much of the work yourself. First, get signed the equity purchase agreement which gives control of the property. After you make the final deal and check the property to make sure that it is in fact transferable, you may personally execute the deed. It is prepared exactly as the previous deed was, then signed by the owners and notarized. As long as the papers are prepared essentially as before and as long as there are no local or state laws to the contrary, you will probably be able to save the legal preparation fees usually charged.

Once the deed has been properly signed, it must be recorded. This seems the easiest part of the whole transaction, involving going to the county recorder's office, paying whatever fees are required, and recording the deed. A good relationship with a title company offers many opportunities to save money here. Sit down with a title officer and discuss what each of you will do during the procedure. You should explain to the officer that you desire to pay only one title policy cost and only one escrow fee even though the property is being bought from one party and sold to another at the same time (if it is). As in any other normal business transaction, this requires negotiating. A point should be that you are going to find some title company to do this, and if this particular company is not agreeable, you will find another company that is. You should mention that you are not transferring the loan to yourself, that the property is being bought subject to the existing loan. However, if you should decide to keep and lease the property, then the loan would be transferred to you and you would pay a transfer fee at that time.

Appraising
The Property

*"Beware of little expenses.
A small leak will sink a great ship"*

—*Benjamin Franklin*

Appraising The Property Prior To Making Offer

There are many ways of evaluating a property before making the final offer. True market value of any property is what the buyer is willing to pay and a seller is willing to take. It is always based on a willing buyer and a willing seller. It is the highest price that a property would sell for on the open market, where the seller is not obligated to sell and they buyer is not obligated buy. This is the value to be thinking of when making an offer. This is the highest value listed on the numbers sheet. The offer made to the owner will be considerably less than this. Once the property is bought, the price asked of potential buyers will be considerably more. The market value is the key value of which all other prices will be based.

The best way to get the true market value of the property being considered is by having a good working relationship with a title company. The title company can give a run-down of comparable value in the chosen area, and it is especially advisable that the company be knowledgeable in this area. Title companies usually know what properties are transferred and they keep their information current. Usually they can tell within a few hundred dollars the sales prices that have occurred in the last six months.

A short report on the property being considered is called a "Property Profile" and most title companies can furnish such a report within 24 hours. To obtain such a report, you must call and ask for Customer Service. Your working relationship with the title company should have produced a "service representative" with whom you can refer to when making your request to the Customer Service department. Of course, you are expected to order your title insurance policies from your title company when such items are eventually needed.

How To Determine Market Value

Every house for sale has an asking price and selling price. To arrive at the selling price, the following information is needed.

1. You must know the square footage and features of the houses for sale in the immediate neighborhood. This involves two sets of inquiries, first to the owners or agents representing the seller, and second, to the tax records to confirm the square footage, number of bedrooms, and baths. A visit to the county tax recorder's office will provide you with the square footage. This information is kept in books and is filled by area and street name. Dividing the asking price by the square footage will give you a price per square foot. Average the houses in your area and then multiply the number of square feet in your house by the average price.

Keep in mind that this is an average price. Extras such as swimming pools, spas, etc. will either add or detract from the average figure. Other things that lower a property's value include only one bathroom, proximity to apartments or commercial properties, heavy traffic, freeway noise, etc.

2. You must know the actual selling price and terms of other houses which have sold in the area. This is a little more difficult to obtain since sellers are often sensitive about what their houses actually sold for. If the asking price is too far above the expected selling price, the chances of attracting a buyer in the correct price range is reduced or eliminated completely.

Many existing homes in Southern California contain added rooms or some type of remodeling for which no permit was obtained. When a homeowner wishes to work on his property, he is required to obtain a building permit. The purpose of the permit is to ensure that the owner or his contractor complies with local building and zoning codes. Some property owners do not obtain a permit out of ignorance or perhaps they want to avoid a property tax increase. Additions made without a permit can be bad news for the seller and can delay the closing of escrow for they buyer.

In some cases the add-ons were so well done that they were almost invisible to the eye. Only an expert would be aware of the fact that any additional construction had been done. In the case of an add-on that was done according to code, it is generally a simple matter to obtain a building permit and call for an inspection. In some cases the building inspector could require that a section of wall be removed to show that it was framed properly and that the electrical wiring was enclosed in conduit, etc. When the add-on is not constructed according to code, anything could be needed from minor reconstruction to total tear down of the add-on.

When the add-on is in violation of Zoning Regulations, there are two alternatives. One is total demolition of the add-on and restoration of the house to its original size. An alternative would be to obtain a zoning variance. Common examples include encroachments into side yards, rear yards, or the addition of a second dwelling unit on a lot zoned for single family use.

Always ask the seller of property that you are buying if there are any known building or zoning code violations on the property. Include a statement to this effect in your offer to purchase and have it signed by the seller.

Be aware of the general condition of other houses in the block. Don't make improvements which are clearly out of keeping with the neighborhood.

Territory Selection

In general it is better to look for an area that is showing signs of growth. In any area of growth, where prices are improving and demand is increasing, you have a better change of making a successful deal. If you are in an area into which people want to move, even a less-than-average deal could be profitable. Finding growing areas is easy. Most local newspapers regularly publish information supplied by government bureaus on the traffic flows on the various roads in every area of your county. But before looking at these figures, you ought to have a general idea of what makes an improving area.

1. **New Construction and Rehabilitation:** Builders, developers, and investors are more than willing to put their money and effort into areas that show signs of growth and improvement. These business people usually spend much of the sources they have to prove to the lenders that the areas in which they are investing in show signs of growth. Lenders themselves have market research departments and accurate information as to what areas are worth investing in. If you see developer money going into an area, you can assume that research has shown it to be growing.

2. **New Branches of Major Banks and Retailers:** Banks, supermarkets, discount stores, and major retailers are usually a step or two ahead. They spend money and call in demographic consultants before they

move to invest in any major addition. Whenever you notice that any of these groups are remodeling or building a new office in an area, you could assume that this area is one you also want to be investing in. This group of business people usually tries to make sure that the area in which they are building is a desirable area to be in.

3. **Neighborhood Spirit:** Usually growing neighborhoods have neighborhood associations and clubs that are always in the news with some activity. The activities could be block dances, parades, special money-raising activities, and the like. The important thing here is that you can tell that the people living in this area like the area and have made up their minds that they will do everything they can to improve it. Spirit like this tends to be a self-fulfilling prophecy.

4. **Negative News Items:** Whenever there is a major fire, disturbance or crime, the newspapers usually devote space to it. If when you are reading your local newspapers, you see that consistently one area has more of this kind of activity, you can mark that down as an area to avoid.

5. **Comparison of Top Choices:** For your final decision, more than likely, you will probably be narrowing your choices down to two or three different neighborhoods. The best way to make the final decision on a territory is to visit these neighborhoods often.

6. **Your Personal Test:** Walk through and visit your top choice areas and ask yourself in which area you feel most comfortable. Which area do you like the most? In which area do you feel the best vibrations? Ninety-nine times out of 100, your own personal judgment will be correct.

7. **Your Own Tour of the Area:** You should schedule in your daily calendar regular times for walking or driving around your area. Note the properties that are for sale and the ones that have been sold. You can notice what real estate agencies do the most business in what section of your territory. You can regularly note what property is for sale by owners. You can notice new construction quickly. You can see any rehabilitation. You will know what roads are being improved and what roads are deteriorating.

8. **Local Newspapers:** Scan the classified ads in your local daily newspapers to get an idea of the changing market. If you notice that the number of homes listed for sale in one part of your territory either expands or contracts dramatically you will know that

substantial change is occurring. These ads usually contain information like necessary down payment, sales price, and condition. You can even find distress sale ads or ads placed by people being forced into foreclosure. Check every kind of newspaper in your area – the Penny Savers, the local throw-aways, the home town newspapers, and the regional papers all are sources of information.

9. **For Rent Ads:** Knowing what properties rent for is an important part of your financial analysis. After you go through the financial information on a particular property and before you conclude any purchase, you should know what you can rent property for if you decide to keep it.

10. **Models and Open Houses:** Most areas generally have a running stream of open houses conducted by real estate brokers. These open houses are usually very well done with agents who have printed information sheets. These information sheets are helpful in telling you what the market price and terms are for that particular type of property at that time.

11. **Properties for Sale:** To keep in touch with the current market in real estate, one of the best things to do is to continually call for information about properties for sale. You are in fact a serious buyer, so you can freely ask questions regarding values, sales prices, and sales terms. This full and accurate information and comparables will let you react instantaneously to a good deal you might find.

Types Of Financing

CONVENTIONAL LOANS

Banks, savings and loan associations, and mutual savings banks are the principal sources of conventional loans. If the loan is not insured, the lender will require the buyer to make a down payment of 20% or more. The larger down payment reduces the risk to the lender in case the buyer defaults at a later date.

INSURED CONVENTIONAL LOANS

A privately-insured conventional loan requires less down payment because a private insurer guarantees repayment of the loan. Buyers are required to make a 10% down payment. Both the buyer and the property must qualify for the loan. The lender will have the house appraised and check the buyer's credit.

FHA LOANS

These are insured loans, if you are considered a candidate. Usually the house is old or located in the "inner city" of a large metropolitan area. This type of loan is obtained by a bank, savings and loan association, or a mortgage banker who writes FHA insured loans in your area. The appraisal can take as long as six weeks. The FHA appraised value will be the maximum amount you can get for your house, unless your new buyer signs a declaration advising that he agrees to pay more then the FHA appraised value. The lender requires an additional fee called "points". One point equals 1% of the loan amount. The FHA requires that the seller pay the points. At one time, the seller could raise the asking price by the value of the points; in this way the buyer was paying the points. Under the present FHA regulations, the house must be appraised at the market value, and the seller pays the points.

A greater number of conventional and insured conventional loans are being made, because it involves less red tape, can be made in a couple of weeks, and is usually less expensive to the buyer and the seller.

Adjustable Rate Mortgages (ARM)

Many people are confused over the different loan rates which are listed in the financial section of the paper. The following information may help.

Question: I've seen many newspaper ads for home loans that show very low interest rates. Are these loans for real or is there a catch?

Answer: Many of these ads are for adjustable rate mortgages. These loans may have low rates for a short period of time but will soon be adjusted upward to the market rate. The interest rate and monthly payment can go up or down depending on various indexes which reflect the cost of money to the lender.

Question: Will I have advance notice of how much my payment may go up?

Answer: With an ARM, your future monthly payment is uncertain; however some types of ARM's will put a ceiling on our payment or rate increase.

Question: How will I know if an ARM is the right type of loan for me?

Answer: This will depend on your financial status and the terms of the

ARM. ARMs carry risks in periods of rising interest rates but can be cheaper over a longer term if interest rates decline. In order to compare one ARM with another you must compare features such as cap rate, percent increase in any one year period, pre payment penalty, negative amortization, and cost of funds index. You must also take into account the maximum amount your monthly payment could increase as well as your future ability to pay.

Question: What are the advantages of an ARM?

Answer: For one, lenders will generally charge lower initial interest rates for ARMs than for fixed rate mortgage; thus, the ARM may be easier on your pocket book at first then a fixed rate loan for the same amount. You may also qualify for a larger loan since lenders often make the decision on the basis of your current income and the first year's payments. If interest rates remain steady or move lower, your ARM could be less expensive over a long period than a fixed rate loan.

Question: What are the disadvantages?

Answer: An increase in interest rates would lead to higher monthly payments in the future. Other considerations include (1) whether or not your income is likely to grow in order to cover higher loan payments should interest rates go up, (2) whether or not you will be assuming other sizable debts such as a car or school tuition in the near future, and (3) the length of time that you plan to own the home. For instance, rising interest rates may pose a problem if you plan to own the house for a long time.

Question: What are adjustment periods?

Answer: With most ARMs, the interest rates and monthly payments change every six months of every year. The period between rate changes is called the adjustment period.

Question: How can I reduce my risk?

Answer: Many ARMs have caps that protect borrowers from extreme increases in interest rates or monthly payments. There are benefits and disadvantages to these caps.

Question: What are interest rate caps?

Answer: An interest rate cap places a limit on the amount of your interest and they come in two versions: (1) period caps, which limit interest rate increases from one adjustment to the next and, (2) overall caps, which limit interest rates over the life of the loan. With some ARMs, payments may increase even if the index rate stays the same or declines. This may occur when your interest rate cap has been holding the interest rate down below the index plus margin.

Question: What is negative amortization?

Answer: If your ARM contains a payment cap, this is an important concept. Negative amortization means that the loan balance is increasing and may occur whenever your monthly payments are not enough to pay all of the interest due on your loan. Since payments caps limit only the payment increase, your rates are not subject to the same protection. Thus, the interest may be charged on that amount.

Question: What is prepayment and conversion?

Answer: After getting an ARM, your financial circumstances may change, and you may decide that you don't want to risk any further changes in your interest rate and payment amount.

(1) Prepayment: Many agreements require a penalty due if you pay off the ARM early. Many ARMs allow you to pay off the loan in full or in part without penalty whenever the rate is adjusted. Pre-payment details are often negotiable and, if so, you may wish to negotiate for no penalty or the smallest one possible.

(2) Conversion: Your agreement with the lender may have a clause that allows you to convert the ARM to a fixed rate after a number of years.

I have only covered the major features of ARMs and I'm sure you will agree that the advice of a competent loan broker or loan officer is a must when considering the best financing terms for you. Another thing to consider is that a property with an ARM will be harder to sell to a future buyer. Another problem with ARMs is that some lenders will look at the high end of the interest spread when dealing with a buyer who wants to assume your ARM. This will effectively shut your buyer out of the market or force you to make a reduction in the sales price.

In summary, an ARM would only appear to make sense if you were planning on a short term holding period or if you were expecting to receive enough funds in the future to pay off the ARM in the event it started to increase faster than your ability to keep up with the payments.

Above all, please avoid any ARM which has a NEGATIVE AMORTIZATION potential. The house you save may be the one you are living in.

Discounting Liens

*"It's choice — not chance —
that determines your destiny."*

—*Jean Nidetch*

Discounting Liens

Except for the first mortgage loan, there is a possibility of removing even second mortgage loans and other liens on the property without paying dollar for dollar. If the loan holder is out of the area and not able to spend the time necessary to take care of the situation, there is a very good chance of getting a discount. The important steps to follow in covering this end of the transaction are.

Get complete information on all mortgages and liens on the property. The information begins with the homeowner, but the most reliable data will come from the county records. All the liens of this kind are on record. All information about them is available. This important point to compile are the date the lien was placed, the amount, the terms, the conditions, the original agreements between the troubled owner and the lien holder. Here again it is very important to check the law in the particular state involved. Most laws are different from state to state in this regard.

It can be shown to a second mortgage lien holder that if he takes over the property, he will have many additional problems. This is done by relating what has been discovered about the neighborhood, essentially the same information as was given to the troubled owner. The same dollars and cents data is used. He would be better off to take a dollar settlement from the investor and concentrate on his other business. After all, he is not in the business of going out and trying to buy properties. He undoubtedly has other investments and this is just another way to put money to work. He should be told how many dollars would be required to bring the loans current, the pitfalls in time and money that await him if he takes his course. A presentation should be given of the problems with the property, the repair work that is needed, and the time and attention that would be necessary to make it happen.

Nobody who puts money out in second and third mortgages really want to buy other people's problems. The liens that are placed by vendors and suppliers are usually desperate moves made in an attempt to salvage something out of a bad business deal. Very few people think they are going to get fifty cents on a dollar with their liens. A lien is a last resort protection move. Therefore, most of them would welcome some kind of effort from someone like the investor who will give them something on their dollars.

By getting in to the habit of negotiating good deals on liens and second mortgages, it is possible to double and triple profit opportunities on each one of the separate purchases.

The property with an existing mortgage on it must be handled with care. Most lenders would like to continually rewrite mortgages, always increasing the interest rate, increasing their yield, and making more and more profit from a particular loan of an existing unit. On the other hand, as a buyer, the investor wants to buy the property subject to the existing loan.

Any information from the lender such as beneficiary statement should be supplied by the troubled owner or by his representative. There should be no expense to the investor in this matter. Many lenders will try to get an additional charge for providing information, but this is part of the service they are required to give the people borrowing from them. Any information regarding the condition of the account, the amount of money owed and other financial matters should be supplied by the lender without additional charge.

Redemptive Rights Of IRS On Junior Liens May Be Negotiable

One governmental agency has the unique right to redeem a property after a property is sold at a trustee's sale. Federal government may redeem from 120 days after the trustee's sale. This time period represents a time when repair or remodeling costs may not be reimbursed by the IRS upon redemption.

IRS liens which have been recorded prior to the date of the recording of the trustee deed being foreclosed upon stay with the property when purchased at the sale. IRS liens recorded after the date of recording of the foreclosing loan are eliminated like other non-priority liens. However, the ability of the IRS to maintain a degree of control of the property after the sale tends to make such purchases less attractive to potential trustees' sale bidders – and therefore inadvertently may tend to deflate potential sales prices of such properties.

Section 7425(d) of the Internal Revenue Code provides that the United States may redeem property sold in a non-judicial proceeding when the sale is made to satisfy a lien prior to that of the Government. However, the District Director for the Internal Revenue District in which the property is located has been delegated authority to release any right to redeem the property.

The government has the option to release its right to redeem the property if the interested party pays the Internal Revenue Service an amount equal to the value of that right. It is possible that the IRS will consider that the right of redemption is valueless and no payment for redemption will be required.

The monetary value of that right apparently varies with the amount of the total junior IRS liens, the potential equity in the property and the costs of redemption, advertising and auction for the IRS. Those rights may be sold for substantially less than the actual amount of the IRS under certain conditions.

The Special Procedures Department of the IRS may be contacted concerning redemptive rights before or after the purchase of a property at a non-judicial foreclosure. The potential or actual purchaser of a property with junior IRS liens may obtain instruction directly from the IRS for preparing an Application Requesting the United States to Release Its Right to Redeem Property Secured by a Federal Tax Lien.

Internal Revenue Service will require the petitioner to give 1) the name and address of the person requesting the United States to release its right for redeem, 2) a description of the property, 3) information about the non-judicial sale, 4) the property owner's name and address at the date of the application, 5) a list of encumbrances and charges, 6) a copy of each Notice and Federal Tax Lien (Form 668) affecting the property, 7) an estimate of the fair market value of the property, 8) any additional information that the petitioner believes would affect the application, 9) any other information requested by the District Director (such as copies of the Notice of Trustee's Sale and the Trustee's deed Upon Sale), 10) a daytime phone number where the petitioner can be reached, and 11) the name, address and phone number of the petitioner's attorney or representative. The petitioner is also required to make the following declaration of his/her signature and title: "Under penalties of perjury, I declare that I have examined this application (including accompanying schedules, exhibits, affidavits, and statements) and to the best of my knowledge and belief it is true, correct and complete." If there is an IRS lien on the property before the property can be sold, a Certificate of Discharge of Property from federal lien must be obtained from the IRS.

Example Of A Trustee State
Charges, Fees And Payment To The Owner

Anytime during the three-month and 16 day reinstatement period after the trustee files a notice of default, you may pay off the delinquent charges and reinstate the loan. These charges include delinquent payments (interest and principal), late charges, costs, and fees incurred during the foreclosure.

The costs or fees include payment for professional services rendered by trustees, attorneys, and other advisors. Costs include cash disbursements for delinquent obligations, such as taxes and debt service, as well as the trustee expenses necessary to foreclose.

Excessive costs are commonly included. These are often simply stated but specifically unaccountable. Since fees are restricted by statute, beneficiaries and trustees often try to include other fees and expenses. To determine if an expense is justifiable, use three guidelines.

1. Were the costs and expenses actually incurred in enforcing the terms of the deed of trust or mortgage?

2. Are there limits on these charges set by state laws?

3. Is there a receipt for the expenditure?

During the three-month and 16 day reinstatement period, only one fee is obtainable (even if both fees are less than the statute maximums). However, if legal expenses are incurred in extra-judicial proceedings connected with the foreclosure, the owner-trustor is obligated to pay them in order to reinstate.

It is absolutely unreasonable to pay fees on costs that were not actually incurred. All costs, including the lender's expenditures for fees, must be justified and reasonable. The more careful you are in your analysis of these expenses, the less overall expenses you will have, and the more profit you will make.

When you are ready to make the final payment to the troubled owners of the property, do it outside the house when they are moving. Never pay them inside the house before they leave. Remember that the deal is not consummated until they have vacated the house totally.

As a prospective buyer, you will also need to be aware of the following legal guidelines relating to the protection of the seller.

Many states, including California, have passed various laws to protect defaulting homeowners from rip-off artists. For instance, the California legislature enacted in 1979, (and amended in 1980), laws restricting the use of so-called Home Equity Sales Contracts.

A Home Equity Sales Contract is any contract involving the purchase of a residence in foreclosure by anyone other than (1) someone purchasing the residence as their personal residence, (2) someone who is a spouse, blood relative, or blood relative of the spouse of the seller, or (3) purchasing by trustees deed, deed in lieu of foreclosure, judgment of court, or sale otherwise authorized by statute.

A residence in foreclosure is any residence consisting of from one to four family dwelling units, one of which the seller occupies as his or her personal residence, that is subject to an outstanding notice of default.

If an investor purchases a residence in foreclosure, then that person must follow the strict guidelines of that legislation or be faced with the possibility of stiff civil and criminal penalties.

For instance, each such contract must be the complete agreement of the parties, must be written in letters of a size equal to 10-point bold type, and must contain the following terms:

1. The name, business address, and telephone number of the purchaser

2. The address of the residence in foreclosure

3. The total consideration to be paid by the purchaser

4. A complete description of the terms of payment or other considerations including, but not limited to, any services of any nature which the purchaser is to perform for the seller before or after the sale

5. The time at which possession is to be transferred

6. The terms of any rental agreement

7. The following notice in the immediate proximity of the space reserved for the seller's signature

Promissory Notes

"The secret of success in life
is for a man to be ready for
his opportunity when it comes."

—*Benjamin Disraeli*

Types Of Promissory Notes

There are three basic types of promissory notes which may be the subject of a trust deed. They are: (1) the straight note, (2) the installment note, and (3) the all-exclusive note.

The straight note is a document which promises to pay the principal sum of the loan in one single payment. Periodic payments of interest may be included in the note or interest may be allowed to accumulate over the term of the loan.

The installment note is a document which provides for periodic payments of principle and, perhaps, interest. An installment note requires at least two payments of principle on different dates. Some installment notes included the payment of interest with each payment of principle. Other types of installment notes, "interest extra," provide for separate additional payments of accumulated interest.

The all-inclusive note, sometimes known as the "wraparound" note is a document which requires the borrower to make payments to the seller which covers both the amount of the carry-back loan as well as the amount due on an underlying or junior note and trustee deed. (From these payments, the seller then makes the monthly payments directly to the lender on the underlying trust deed). The benefit of using an all-exclusive note is that sometimes the seller is able to obtain interest on the money he never loaned to the borrower. The disadvantage to the borrower is that he may be paying higher interest than if he assumed the underlying note and trust deed.

The terms of all three types of promissory notes may be negotiated and are generally not fixed by law. Remember, just because a legal document is presented in a preprinted form, does not mean that its terms cannot be changed or deleted.

In all three types of promissory notes, both the borrower and lender should be aware of the presence or absence of an "or more" clause. The inclusion of this clause permits the borrower to prepay the note at anytime without permission from the lender. If they "or more" clause is not contained in the note, then without the lender's permission the borrower may not prepay the note. (There are some exceptions to this rule, particularly in the area of residential property of less than five units).

If a lender wants to sell of transfer his interest in a note and trust deed to another party, he may accomplish this by completing a document known as an "assignment". This document is generally less than one page long and states that the note and deed of trust are being immediately assigned to someone else. To be safe, the person acquiring the note and deed of trust should record the assignment.

On May 28, 1985, in Baypoint vs. Crest, the California Court of Appeal made a new law by judicial fiat, holding, in general, that if a promissory note has a late charge provision; one cannot foreclose under the deed of trust until after the late charge has been accrued. Typically, late charges and promissory notes are only valid if they come into effect at least 11 days following the date that the installment is due. In the Baypoint case, the promissory notes the provided that if the payment is not received within 10 days from the due date, the lender could impose a 10% late charge on the installment. Since the borrower was habitually late in making his payments under 23 separate promissory notes, the lender, as an inducement to have the borrower pay in a timely manner, initiated a foreclosure prior to the expiration of the 10 days. (Presumably, the lender believed that trustees' fees for handling the foreclosure of $15,000 each time the borrower was late would be ample encouragement for him to make timely payments.)

The court held that a lender may not use the foreclosure procedure to encourage borrowers to make timely payments until the late charge had been incurred.

Promissory notes, trust deeds and foreclosures are the subject of highly technical law which gives rise to all sorts of legal pitfalls. It is always best to consult with someone knowledgeable in this field prior to taking specific action.

Key Points To Remember About Existing Mortgages

You should get into the habit of discounting liens and mortgages on properties. Since more liens and mortgages are untroubled property, you have a great opportunity to make a bigger profit. The more complicated the deal, the more ammunition you have to explain to the lienholders the various problems and tell them they have a one-shot opportunity to get out with something. That opportunity is by dealing with you. The more problems involved in a property in your selected area, the greater your chance.

Handle the property with an existing mortgage on it with care. Most lenders would like to continually rewrite mortgages, always increasing the interest rate, increasing their yield, and making more and more profit from a particular loan on an existing unit. On the other hand, as a buyer, you want to buy the property subject to the existing loan so you could get the benefit of the older interest rate and lower monthly payments. All this is possible in most states. The important thing to remember is that it requires great care and concern for details. Federal savings and loans can enforce due on sale clauses and requires special care.

1. Always assume that the lender would like to rewrite the mortgage at a higher interest rate with larger monthly payments and be very careful to do everything correctly when acquiring property.

2. Never use the term "assuming" in a purchase. Always say you are taking title "subject to". An assumption gives the lender control over your deal. Even when you purchase an FHA or GI mortgage property, for all practical purposes, avoid the word "assumption".

3. Any property with an existing conventional loan from a non federal savings and loan can be purchases subject to the existing loan, unless specific laws say otherwise.

4. The buyer of the property must be concerned only with the seller's equity or the seller's obligations in addition to the first mortgage.

5. You can pay cash above the loan, or part cash and execute a note and second mortgage for the balance of the seller's equity. But in any case, whenever you can take over the property subject to the existing loan you will benefit.

6. Avoid land contracts or other security devices.

7. Credit reports are not necessary to transfer title. In this situation, the lender does not have to approve the new buyer's credit. Once the lender gets involved, his first effort will be to try to rewrite the mortgage at a higher interest rate.

8. No reinspection or recertification of the property is required when the property is transferred in this manner.

9. Closing, transferring title, or passing escrow becomes very easy in sales of this type. All you need is to pass the deed and pay the money.

Balloon Payment — What To Do When Creative Financing Plans Come Due At Last

Buyers, sellers, and agents are concerned about the time when the creative financing comes due; will the buyers be able to buy off the loan, the large balloon payment, or will they lose the home?

The seller is concerned because he eventually may have a house back, and have to make payments one a first trust deed. Agents are concerned because they put the deal together and want things to work out well.

There are several ways to resolve the problem, both at the time the contract of purchase is written up, and when the loan becomes due and payable.

Preventive measures are best. When the contract is made, set up the pay off for as long a time away as is possible. Years ago, three years was the most common length of time for paybacks, but that isn't long enough today. Five years is better, and seven years is even better.

A lot of listings have 10-year due dates. It gives the buyer the opportunity to accumulate money to pay off the loan as well as allowing sufficient time for equity build-up for refinancing. To make the 10-year due date more palatable for the seller (who may need the money), write into the contract periodic interest increases and/or periodic sums of money to be paid off in a lump sum. For instance, the seller carries back a second trust deed for 10 years and there is an interest increase every two years. Or the buyer will pay off one-tenth of the original amount of the loan every two years. There are innumerable ways to work out the problem to please both the buyer and seller. Another preventive step is to write into the contract an extension of the loan, probably with different terms, to eliminate any problems at the time the loan is due and payable.

If preventive measures weren't taken, there are five main alternatives to consider when the loan becomes due:

1. **Pay off the loan when it becomes due:** Of course, this implies the borrower has the money to pay it off. This can be planned for with a meaningful savings plan.

2. **Extend the loan:** If an automatic extension wasn't written in at the beginning, you can contact the seller four to six months before the loan becomes due and try to extend it. Even if you try to do it initially there is not harm in trying again. Frequently, the lender (the original seller) gets the lump sum (there are times when this may mean an increase of payment to the government). Propose it with an interest increase to make it more palatable.

3. **Get a new second trust deed:** If the borrower can't afford to pay off the loan and the holder of the loan needs the money and won't extend it, then get another second trust deed. You can always go to commercial lenders, but friends and relatives may be more than willing to assist you and earn interest at the same time. If you go this route, be sure you make it business-like so you do not ruin the relationship. You can also consider an equity-sharing arrangement.

4. **Sell the house:** This can be an especially good idea if the mortgage rates have dropped or remained the same. This option permits the borrower to get out some of the equity build-up in the property, thereby releasing cash for other uses.

5. **Refinance the entire mortgage:** This can be an especially good idea if the mortgage rates have dropped or remained the same. This option permits the borrower to get out some of the equity build-up in the property, thereby releasing cash for other uses.

Whichever option you select (other than paying off the loan with savings,) allow yourself plenty of time. Beginning a year before might not be too early in this market.

"2 Plus 3 Rule"

As a rule of thumb, to decide whether refinancing will pay off, ask yourself these questions:

1. Are you going to stay in your property another three years?

2. Is the new mortgage interest at least two percentage points lower than your present rate?

If you can answer yes to the above, you will probably come out ahead. Ask the lender to tell you what your new monthly payments will be and to give you a rundown of closing costs.

"Do the arithmetic"

Refinancing

Benefits of refinancing your existing home mortgage, depends on a variety of factors.

Don't forget the 2 + 3 rules. You will be charged points and fees—between 1 and 2 percentage points of the amount borrowed—plus closing costs and other fees; this is the cost of buying the new loan.

In refinancing and adjustable-rate mortgage, consider the interest rate cap. If the starting interest rate and the interest rate cap on the new loan both are lower than your old adjustable-rate loan, you have a good deal.

In shopping for an adjustable-rate mortgage, look at the different caps (maximum rate the loan can ever increase). Does the mortgage you are considering have cap or ceiling on the interest rate or is there a cap on the dollar amount of the payment? Mortgages with payment caps that are exercised can lead to deferred interest, causing your mortgage balance to increase.

The lower the locked-in interest start-rate, the lower the interest cap or ceiling is. Good protection against possible future increases in the inflation rate.

The cost of buying a new loan must be amortized over time and compared with your new monthly payment and savings. Is there an overall cost savings to you?

Selling Techniques

"Entrepreneurs are simply those who understand that there is little difference between obstacle and opportunity and are able to turn both to their advantage."

—Victor Kiam

How To Start Selling

Every year, thousands of homeowners sell their homes without a real estate agent and pocket the real estate commission. You can save thousands of dollars in the process.

The system of home transfer is one of the most costly exchanges to be found anywhere. The combination of transfer fees and brokerage fees take a huge toll from the seller. The largest of these fees is the brokerage commission (about 6% of the selling price).

"FOR SALE BY OWNER" is a phrase that real estate agents and brokers refer to as *FSBO (pronounced "fizbow")*. This phrase can bring people to the property because everybody is looking for a chance to save on commissions.

Some of the services in selling a house can be purchased from other professionals and the balance can be performed by you.

California is escrow minded. It is not necessary to use an escrow company in selling a house. You can set up a trust account in a bank, the funds to be disbursed when the transaction is completed. A competent lawyer will take care of many of the details involved in a home sale.

You are more motivated than a broker or anyone else to sell your house. You can make selling your home a rewarding and satisfactory experience.

Selling Your House

- Don't get emotionally involved with your house. Fix up what is necessary.

- The house that sizzles sells the fastest.

- Make sure the outside looks neat and trim.

- Hose the outside down a few hours before you have open house. Everything looks and smells nice.

- Painting does wonders, always use neutral colors. Perhaps just a trim on the outside is needed.

- Potted plants around the patio or pool area makes a difference.

- If there is a fireplace and it's cold outside, have a crackling fire.

- Put some vanilla extract in the oven for a few minutes; the house will smell divine.

- Give the owners or tenants some lunch money the day of the open house. Emotionally, it's best for the owners not to be present when showing it to future buyers.

- As soon as you buy a house, put a "For Sale By Owner" sign outside the house. Make sure you have your telephone number on it.

- Having an answering service is important in this business. Place an ad in any of your local newspaper and qualify your people over the telephone.

- Ad should be placed under the city in which the property is in.

- Buyers like to buy home from private parties because they know they can save a broker's commission.

- Don't forget to have fire insurance.

Advertising In Local Papers

- The best media in which to advertise a home are local newspapers. This includes the regional paper, the local paper and the weekly throw-a ways.

Anything that is printed and distributed in the area is a source for good ad response. The point is to maximize the dollar. The investor should sit down and ask himself what he would like to read if he was looking for a home.

• The headline for the ad should always read "For Sale By Owner." This is a magic phrase. Everybody is looking to get something by saving commissions. Since the investor is not a real estate agent, it is not necessary to put down owner agent. He is an independent principal selling his own home.

• Always start out the ad copy by saying "Newly Decorated" and fill in blanks, three bedrooms, four bedrooms, two or three baths.

• Always put down the sale price.

• State that it is available for immediate occupancy.

For Sale By Owner

Newly decorated 3 BR home (Address). Sale price $_____.
Principals only (time and phone number to call).

1. Put address of property and your phone number in ad.

2. Put "For Sale" sign on property and include your phone number.

3. Put ad in the classified section of the newspaper under homes for sale and under the city which the property is located.

4. Use local papers for selling your home.

Preparing Your House For Sale

How much work should you do before you put your house on the property market; and will it really increase the value of your property? There are a number of repairs and renovations that will increase the selling price of your house, but there are other upgrades that probably won't return their cost. First, hire a professional cleaning service to come in and give the place a thorough cleaning. Then check the following areas:

1. **Walls:** New wallpaper will add little to the selling price; the new owner has his own idea on color and design.

2. **Floors:** Don't replace the old carpeting. Have existing carpet cleaned and apply a coat of wax to the hard wood or linoleum.

3. **Exterior:** A new roof might improve the appearance, but leave it alone unless water is actually leaking through the ceiling.

4. **Landscaping:** Don't place expensive new rosebushes in anticipation of a gardener moving in. Remove all weeds and give the yard a good clean up.

In general, the rule is to clean it rather then replace or redo. Do only those repairs which are safety-related. Don't try to anticipate the decorating tastes of your buyers. Be aware of the general condition of the other houses on the block. Don't make improvements which are clearly out of keeping with the neighborhood.

Preparing Your Home For Showing

With buyers, first impressions count. A small investment in time and money will give your home an edge over other listings in the area when the time comes to show it to a prospective buyer. Here are some suggestions that will help you to get top market value:

General Maintenance
• Oil squeaky doors
• Tighten doorknobs
• Replace burned out lights
• Clean and repair windows
• Touch up chipped paint
• Repair cracked plaster
• Repair leaking taps and toilets

Spic And Span
• Shampoo carpets
• Clean washer, dryer, and tubs
• Clean furnace
• Clean fridge and stove
• Clean and freshen bathrooms

The First Impression
• Clean and tidy entrance
• Functional doorbell
• Polish door hardware

Curb Appeal
• Cut lawns
• Trim shrubs and lawns
• Weed and edge gardens
• Pick up any litter
• Clear walk and driveway of leaves
• Repair gutters and leaves
• Touch up exterior paint

The Buying Atmosphere
• Be absent during showings
• Turn on all lights
• Light fireplace
• Open drapes in the day time
• Play quiet background music
• Keep pets outdoors

The Spacious Look
• Clear stairs
• Store excess furniture
• Clear counters and stove
• Make closets neat and tidy

How To Make A Good First Impression

The condition of your house is a key factor in selling it. Put yourself in the place of a potential buyer, drive past your house; do you find it attractive enough to stop and look further? House buyers shop the market and compare value.

TIPS FOR SHOWCASING YOUR HOUSE

1. Trim and green your front and back lawn. Flowers add color and are very attractive.

2. Check out all electrical equipment. Make sure the door bell works and that the front door has no cracked or chipped paint.

3. Painting will give a fresh look to the inside and out. Sometimes all that is needed on the outside is a trim.

4. Clean or replace the carpeting if badly worn. Keep the color in the neutral family. The inside of the house should be painted "NAVAJO WHITE".

5. Replace light bulbs as needed. The lighter the house is, the more cheerful it looks.

6. Wash and repair windows if needed. A view of the yard makes the house look larger.

7. Kitchen and bathrooms are most important to potential buyers. Cleanliness is the key element. Put a little vanilla extract in the oven for a delightful smell. Logs burning in the fireplace produce a cozy affect in the winter months.

8. Real plants and fresh flowers in a vase can do wonders for an empty room.

Be prepared to discuss all of your appliances. Know the brand names and know if there are warranties in affect on any of the appliances (and if there are, have the warranties available).

Make sure you know about the local schools, the major shopping centers, freeways, and any other features that may be of interest to your prospect. Be familiar with all of the special features of your neighborhood and community. Your Chamber of Commerce will supply you with important information for your community. "Knowing the territory" is the best attribute of any good sales person.

Good Salesmanship

To be successful in selling your house, follow these rules of good salesmanship:

1. Show self-confidence. Don't dress too formal, but do be neat and clean.

2. Be enthusiastic. The possibility of upgrading their standard of living is an exciting experience and you must share this experience with the buyer.

3. Smile! Make the buyer feel at home. Be patient, objective and logical. Emotions will confuse a successful negotiation.

4. All offers should be examined. An outright decline may not be in your best interest. Consider a counter offer which is reasonable and likely to close the gap between the buyer and you.

5. Try to close the sale without too much delay. A serious buyer will cool off if too much time elapses.

6. When an agreement is reached, get it in writing. A sales agreement form, available in most stationary stores, should be used to cover all details of the sales.

7. Obtain earnest money upon the signing of the sales agreement. This can help psychologically.

Your first contact with your prospect might be on the telephone. Put a smile in your voice when you answer the telephone. Ask the person's name so that you can refer to it as you respond. Don't oversell. Ask what time they would like to see the house. Use the same advertising techniques on the telephone that you use in writing your ad. Get his attention.

Don't let the prospects wander through the house alone. You should always guide them on the tour. Pre-arrange the tour to emphasize the best features of your house at the beginning and end of the tour. If there are negatives, show them in between.

Ask the right questions. Ask where the prospect lives and why he is interested in moving in moving. Ask those questions that require a positive response. Only ask a few questions; don't pry into personal lives. Observe his responses carefully. Asking questions helps you avoid talking too much. You should be a good listener, and by asking questions you will avoid overselling.

Overcoming Objections

A good salesperson has no fear of objections. The buyer who raises objections is probably thinking seriously about purchasing your house. Many of these objections will not be real; they are symptoms of the caution they feel must be exercised in making an important decision. Be prepared for these objections by comparing your house with other houses.

The following are ways to handle objections:

1. Make the objections appear minor in relation to the other qualities of the house. Don't dwell on the objection. Nod your head in agreement and change the subject.

2. Never lie or argue with the prospect. Do not give them any reason to mistrust you.

3. Always listen very carefully to the prospect's objections. Don't avoid the question. These objections may be the key to your sale.

4. Know when to stop selling and start closing.

5. Request a contract and earnest money.

Once the prospect makes affirmative statements such as "it looks pretty good," you have reached the point where you should stop selling. Your prospect is making a mental commitment and you should stop selling and start closing.

Your next step is to settle on the price and work out the details. Both seller and buyer should go to the closing thinking they got the best deal possible.

Guidelines To Opening An Escrow

To open escrow, deliver to your escrow holder the following information:

1. Buyer's name and vesting (how buyer will take title)

2. Buyer's present address, home phone number and office number and/or message number

3. Seller's name

4. Seller's present address, if not property address, and home phone number and office number and/or message number

5. Address of property - house number, including Avenue, Street, Lane, etc., and Zip Code

6. City

7. As much of legal description and parcel number as possible

8. FINANCING:

    A. NEW LOAN
       1. Amount
       2. Name, address, phone number and name of loan agent
       3. Interest rate
       4. Loan fee

    B. SECONDARY FINANCING
       1. Amount
       2. Interest rate
       3. Due date
       4. Late charges
       5. Acceleration clause
       6. Request for Notice of Default
       7. Name, address, phone number and name of loan agent if not purchase money

    C. ASSUMPTION OF EXISTING LOAN
       1. Amount of approximate unpaid balance
       2. Name, address, and loan number of existing Lender
       3. Interest rate - will it remain the same or be adjusted?
       4. Loan assumption fees and/or charges assessed by existing lender

    D. LAND CONTRACT OR ALL-INCLUSIVE
       1. Name(s) of underlying beneficiary(s) and approximate unpaid balances(s)
       2. Principal amount of Land Contract of All-Inclusive Note/Trust Deed
       3. Interest rate
       4. Due date

5. Late charges
6. Request for Notice of Default
7.   Acceleration clause
8. Special terms or conditions

E. ADVISE THAT PARTIES SEEK LEGAL ADVICE
1. Name(s), address(s), and loan number(s) of any loan(s) or encumbrance(s) to paid off at the close of escrow.
2. Specific contingency(s) or conditions which escrow is subject to and the date said contingency(s) shall expire and be deemed approved.
3. Smoke Detectors. Check with the Department of Building and Safety for City Ordinance and party responsible for installation of smoke detectors.
4. Termite Inspection Report, if applicable.
5. Additional instructions pursuant to sale no mentioned above.

F. MEMO ITEMS AGREED UPON BETWEEN BUYER AND SELLER OUTSIDE OF ESCROW'S JURISDICTION
1. Personal property; e.g., window treatment, fireplace equipment, etc.
2. Warranties
3. Date of possession to Buyer

G. FIRE INSURANCE *(assume existing or new policy)*
1. Name of agent and insurance company, phone number, policy number (if assumed) and verification to escrow holder if property located in a brush area that may require California Fair Plan to write policy.

H. CONDOMINIUMS ONLY *(provide name and address of homeowners association and amount of monthly dues)*
1. Name of Title Company and representative to credit order.
2. Preliminary Chance of Ownership Form – make sure form is filled in completely and signed by County Recorder.

Take Note

If the Seller is a widow or widower – has or will property be probated? If not subject to probate, escrow holder will probably need Affidavit of Death of Joint Tenant and/or Inheritance Tax Lien Release.

If Seller is in title as a married man, a married woman or no status spouse may need to execute a Quitclaim Deed, or participate in transaction as a Seller.

If Buyer is to acquire title as a marred man, as his sole and separate property, or a married woman, as her sole and separate property, spouse will have to execute a Quitclaim Deed.

If Seller holds title as Trustee for a Living Trust, or if Buyer is to acquire title as Trustee of Living Trust: Title Company and/or Lender may require copies of Trust, and a statement from Trustee that Trust is still in effect and has not been amended.

If a parent and child (over 18) are to acquire title in any combination, that relationship will be stated in addition to material status.

If Seller is reselling property within one year, did they acquire it with a binder. If so, title policy must be obtained through original issuing title company.

If you do not know Buyer's vesting, no Grant Deed can be drawn.

In the event property is in a brush area, allow six (6) weeks for fire insurance policy. Advise escrow early in the transaction.

Any inquires to escrow holder must be made by a Principal to the transaction or their Real Estate Agents. Buyer's or Seller's attorneys, accountants, ex-wives are not entitled to information without clear direction from principal.

The Interim Binder

The Interim Binder is a form of title insurance designed to save money on the title insurance costs for those purchasers who intend to hold property for two years or less.

If you are not aware of the benefits a binder provides, they are:

Question: How does a binder save a purchaser money?

Answer: A binder provides a means to insure title to the property and receive a discount when that land is sold.

Question: How does a binder work?

Answer: At the time of purchase, the seller pays the normal fee for the buyer's title policy and the buyer pays an additional 10%. When the buyer sells the property within two years, he only has to pay for any additional amount of the sales price over the original amount of the binder.

Question: What happens if my buyer decides to keep the property longer than two years?

Answer: After two years, the binder converts to a standard owner's policy of title insurance.

Another option for the insured is to extend his binder for an additional two year period by paying another 10% fee. This can come in very handy if your buyer decides to hold onto the property because of high interest rates, a weak market or some other factor.

Deeds

*"Success is when your
name is in everything
but the phone book."*

—*Unknown*

How To Hold Title To The Property

The best way to hold title to property can be one of the most confusing decisions a buyer of real estate must make. Should we hold title as joint tenants? Community property? Or is there a third, better way?

FOR A HUSBAND AND WIFE

A husband and wife can hold title to property as JOINT TENANTS, COMMUNITY PROPERTY, TRUSTEES OF A REVOCABLE LIVING TRUST, or as their SOLE AND SEPARATE PROPERTY.

JOINT TENANCY

The only advantage to holding title as joint tenants is that it will avoid probate upon the death of the spouse. There are, however, many disadvantages. First, it will NOT avoid probate upon the death of the second spouse. If the property is left to the children, they will have to probate the property. Second, the property does not get a full step up of basis upon the death of one spouse. This means that a surviving spouse may be required to pay capital gains tax if he or she sells the property after death of the first spouse. The capital gains tax could be completely avoided by holding property either as community property or as trustees of a Revocable Living Trust.

COMMUNITY PROPERTY

The advantage of holding title as community property is that the property gets a full step up of basis upon the death of one spouse. This means that if the other spouse sells the property shortly after the death of the first spouse, there will be no capital gains tax, even though the property may have greatly appreciated in value. The disadvantage is that, upon the death of the surviving spouse, the property must go through probate.

REVOCABLE LIVING TRUST

A Revocable Living Trust is a way to hold title to property so that you keep absolute control during your lifetime but, upon your death, title to the property passes automatically as you have designated, completely bypassing the probate system. The Revocable Living Trust is an alternative to a will.

TRUSTEE OF A REVOCABLE LIVING TRUST

Advantages are as follows:

1. No probate when the first spouse dies

2. No probate when the surviving spouse dies

3. The property is not subject to the debts of the kids

4. You maintain complete control of the property

5. The property gets a full step up in basis

6. You have income and estate taxes

The disadvantage is the cost of setting up a Revocable Living Trust. However, in the long run, a tremendous amount of money can be saved.

Question: Does one give up any control of assets by holding title as trustees of a Revocable Living Trust?

Answer: No. You maintain total and absolute control and can buy, sell, lease, and borrow against the property, just the same as before you put it into trust.

Question: Can one Revocable Living Trust be used for all assets?

Answer: Yes. All assets owned by a single person or by a husband and wife can be placed into a Revocable Living Trust. This includes real estate, stocks, businesses, and bank accounts.

Question: Should property owned in another state be put into a Revocable Living Trust?

Answer: Yes, absolutely. If out-of-state property is not put into a Revocable Living Trust, then separate probate must be opened in each state in which you own property. This can result in an expensive and time consuming situation for the heirs.

Question: Is maintaining a Revocable Living Trust expensive?

Answer: No. Most people are the trustees of their Revocable Living Trust during their lifetime. Therefore, there are no additional expenses because of the trust. If the heirs—for example, the children—are named as successor trustees, there would be no trustee fees, even after your death.

Question: Will transferring property into a Revocable Living Trust increase my taxes?

Answer: No. Revenue and Taxation Code Section 62 provides that a transfer into a Revocable Living Trust is exempt from reassessment, so your property taxes will remain the same, per Proposition 13.

PROBATE

Probate is a legal procedure in which the Superior Court assumes control over the assets of someone who has died. The Court supervises the payment of taxes, debts, probate fees, and supervises the distribution of the estate. Unfortunately, the heirs pay a high price in time and money for this service. The assets ate tied up for periods of time ranging from nine months to three years, or more. The cost of probate is estimated to be four to ten percent of the GROSS value of the estate.

STEP-UP IN BASIS

The "basis" of a property is the figure used by the IRS to compute gain or loss on a transaction. Normally, basis is the purchase price. However, when property is inherited through certain ways, the property gets a STEP UP IN BASIS. This means that the value of the property, as of the date of the death of the person who left it to you, is the value used to compute gain. For example, lets assume a man purchased a piece of property for $10,000 in 1910 and it was worth $1,000,000 when he died. If the heirs of that man received the property as an inheritance, then the basis of the property would be $1,000,000. This means that if the heirs sold the property for $1,000,000 there would be no capital gains tax. If the heirs received the property as a GIFT, then the basis would still be $10,000 and the heirs would pay about $198,000 in capital gains tax when they sold it.

In the case of a husband and wife, if they hold title to their property as joint tenants they do not get a full step up in basis; they only get a one-half step up of basis. This means that some capital gains tax could be do upon a sale of the property that occurs after the death of the first spouse. If the property is held as community property or as trustees of a Revocable Living Trust, then the entire property gets a full step up in basis. Holding property as joint tenants can often be a tax trap.

THE BEST WAY

Holding title as trustees of a Revocable Living Trust is the best way to hold title. For a husband and wife, it will eliminate probate fees, get a full step up in basis, and it can save estate taxes. For a single person, holding title as trustee of a Revocable Living Trust allows him/her to have total and absolute control of the property and assures that the heirs receive the property without probate.

Holding title as trustee of a Revocable Living Trust should be considered by everyone when they decide how to take title to property.

Joint Ownership Can Take an Unfriendly Turn

Joint ownership use to be a question for married couples only. But now everyone's getting in to the act. Couples living together, neighbors, parents and children—all are buying various types of property together to divide the cost. Is sharing property a good idea?

FOR FRIENDS

You may decide to buy a boat or vacation house jointly with a friend because neither of you can afford it alone. You arrange to use the boater house on alternate weekends and split the cost of expenses. These arrangements can work if both partners work at it, but these types of plans are very risky. What if you want to sell the boat and your partner does not? What if your partner accidentally damages the property? What if his creditors attach the property? What if your friendship fades?

Co-owners should draw up a detailed contract that covers of all of the "what ifs" and should take out life insurance policies on each other so each can afford to buy the others share if he/she dies. Otherwise, that share will pass to a stranger who you may or may not be able to get along with.

FOR UNMARRIED COUPLES

In short-term relationships, joint ownership isn't even worth talking about. The impulse arises in long-term parings, in which the argument for equitable economic arrangements can be the same as for married couples. If you want to own a house, a dual investment is probably needed to make the down payment. You can own as "tenants in common", which allows each of you to sell or bequeath your share of the property to anyone you choose. Or, you can own as "joint tenants with right of survivorship". The latter lets you sell your share to another party during your life time. If you die, it automatically passes to your co-owner. You might write a contract providing that neither of you will sell his/her share without the other's permission.

In general, the risks of property sharing overwhelm the emotional rewards. If the relationship sours, it may be hard to get your share of the property back. Your partner could clean out a jointly-held bank account. If he/she leaves, he could sell his half of a jointly-held property to a stranger, or threaten to do so in order to pressure you into selling the house. If he dies without a will and you have no right of survivorship, his half will pass to his relatives who might force you out. The property is subject to the claims of either party's creditors. If the reason for joint ownership is to ensure that your partner gets the property at your death, do it instead of writing a proper will.

FOR PARENTS AND CHILDREN

An elderly parent might find it convenient to put an adult child's name on his bank or mortgage account if the child is helping to manage the finances. But, if the child gets into financial trouble, a lien could be put against the joint property and untangling it would be a mess. Also, the child could take the money and run.

The joint property would normally pass to that child at your death, which might bring on a lawsuit if your other children are thereby cut out. A better system might be to give your child power of attorney over your affairs, but leave the property in your own name.

FOR MARRIED COUPLES

Married couples are a lot touchier about jointly owned property than they use to be. Many of them just plain don't like it. For women, separate property has become a symbol of financial independence. For men, it suggests freedom from long-term obligations if the marriage breaks up.

Ironically, just when joint property has become emotionally suspect, it is starting to make better sense under the law. For example, it used to be that jointly-owned bank accounts or safe-deposit boxes were frozen when one spouse died; money was often tied up for months. Now, however, banks are giving surviving spouses the access to joint accounts which they need to pay their bills and keep up the household. Each of you might want to have a modest amount of money in separate names, just in case difficulties arise. But, frozen bank accounts are not longer good arguments for keeping property separate.

Here's another example: many spouses used to face a tax on joint property when the other spouse died. That's no longer true. In fact, at present, the case for jointly-owned assets in your marriage seems to be very strong for the following five reasons:

1. You get the other half of the joint property automatically when your spouse dies. There is no need to go through probate, which will certainly save some money.

2. If your spouse dies owning money, the creditors cannot normally put a lien against joint property that has passed to you (unless you also signed the debts).

3. If you hold real estate in another state, joint ownership saves you from going through probate there.

4. The marriage becomes at true economic partnership; share and share alike.

5. Joint ownership protects the interests of both partners in case of divorce. In most states, marital property can now be divided equally (or unequally, as the courts decide), regardless of who holds formal title. But out-of-state bargaining power is stronger if your name is on everything.

You might take this last point as an argument for separately-held property. But remember this: you would have to hold 50% of the marital property in your own name to equal the interest you would get from joint property. In the nine community-property states, you get many of the advantages of joint property automatically. In fact, you will need legal help if you decide that you want to hold some property separately rather than together.

I can think of only five situations when joint property might cause problems for married couples:

1. Your spouse is vulnerable to court judgments. Creditors could file a lien against the joint property, and even though your share normally can't be seized, it's complicated to get your money our. Depending on state law, the creditor might force the sale of a jointly-owned house to get at the spouse's half. In this case, the non-vulnerable spouse would do better to hold

2. Property in his or her separate name. Even then, you're courting a lawsuit if you transfer property to evade paying a judgment.

3. You have a net worth above $500,000. This makes you liable for federal estate taxes, which can be avoided if each spouse holds the same property separately and leaves it in trust.

4. You have children from a prior marriage. If you put everything into joint names with your new spouse and then die, the spouse inherits everything—and he or she may not provide for your children. To guarantee their inheritance, keep your property separate and leave it to them by will.

5. If a house is your chief asset, joint ownership may be convenient. In this case, consider providing for your children by naming them beneficiaries of your life insurance policy.

Profits In Your Pocket

Question: Which entity should I use to hold my Primary Residence?

Answer: It is never a good idea to hold your personal residence in a business entity such as a corporation or a limited liability company. It prevents you from writing-off mortgage interest and it could cause additional taxing consequences when you want to sell the property. One option is to hold your personal residence in a Living Trust.

Question: Should you ever use a Limited Partnership to hold property?

Answer: A limited partnership is a great estate planning tool. If you plan on holding onto your property for a while and passing it onto your heirs then it would be wise to look at holding the property in a limited partnership (LP). When structured correctly an LP can assist in the elimination of probate, saving your heirs thousands of dollars.

Question: Where should I incorporate?

Answer: The general rule of thumb is that you should form your business entity in the state in which you are doing business. In some cases you may want to look at forming an additional entity in a preferred state like Nevada, due to the limited regulatory requirements, minimal taxes and additional asset protection for the officers and directors.

Question: Should I hold income property in a Limited Liability Company?

Answer: If you are purchasing an income property where you are going to have the additional liability risk of housing renters then It might be a good idea to hold the property in a Limited Liability Company (LLC). Not only will you establish a layer of protection against other business or property interests if you were to be sued but you can also sell the property without any additional tax consequences.

Question: Is there any way to avoid AB 2065, a 3.33% tax on income property?

Answer: The tax requires buyers of income property to withhold 3.33% of the purchase price and pay that money to the Franchise Tax Board. There are only a few exemptions, 1.) If the property is your primary residence. 2.) Sales of $100,000 or less. 3.) If the seller is a California Corporation or a partnership.

Question: What is the best entity for holding properties if you only plan to hold onto the property short-term?

Answer: No matter how long you hold a piece of property you are placing
your other assets at risk, so it is always a good idea to look
at owning the property inside a business entity such as an LLC
of an S-corporation. If you are the sole person involved with the
transaction then you might want to look at using an S-
corporation. If there was more than one person involved then
you should look at using and LLC. Both provide asset protection
and pass through taxation, one is more geared toward multiple
owners while the other provides additional protection to a
single shareholder.

Trustee Sales

*"It is uncommon
to use common sense"*

—*Cleo Katz*

After The Notice Of Sale Is Filed

The Notice of Sale must be recorded and published in a paper of general circulation in the area in which the property is located. The notice is published once a week for the three weeks before the scheduled date of sale. Most Notices of Sale are published in the same legal papers which carry the Notices of Default. Others are published in small rural newspapers which may have cheaper rates, and yet are still close enough to the property to qualify as a permissible source for publication.

The Notice of Sale contains much of the same information that was in the Notice of Default such as the following:

1. The address which the documents are mailed

2. Recording data to locate the original document

3. Source to contact to get an update on the opening bid

4. Name of the Trustee

5. Date of the Deed of Trust that's in default

6. Name of the original Trustor. This may not be the same as the present owner if the property was sold "subject to" the loan.

7. Recording data to locate the original Deed of Trust

8. Original amount of the Deed of Trust in default

9. Legal description of the property

Additionally, the Notice of Sale contains this information:

1. Loan number, to be referred to when contacting the lender

2. Name, address, and phone number of the Trustee holding the sale

3. The amount owing, plus all advances and expenses up the date of recordation

4. Phone number of contact point to determine the opening bid

5. Date, time, and place of sale

After The Sale

Let's assume that you chose not to bid at the sale, or that you were overbid at the sale. Who are the other likely bidders at the sale? The opening bid is made of behalf of the beneficiary to the amount due to him. If there are other bidders, they will undoubtedly become investors, since it is unlikely that a junior lienholder would wait for the sale to protect his interest in the property. He would be more likely to cure the default after the Notice of Default was field and then foreclose into ownership.

It may be possible, therefore, to make a deal with the successful bidder. If you can structure a quick profit for him by cranking cash out of the property and giving him part of his profit in a note, he may go for it. This does not work often enough to plan on it.

In most cases that I have seen, if the cash required at the sale is substantial, there ARE no other bidders and the property is sold to the foreclosing beneficiary.

There are two types of beneficiaries:

1. Private, such as sellers who carried back a note; or investors, who lend on second Deeds of Trust of deal in discounted Deeds of Trust.

2. Institutional, such as banks, savings, and loans, finance companies, credit unions, mortgage companies, etc.

Making Money While Helping Others Out Of Trouble

TRUSTEE SALES/AUCTIONS

Formally called Trustee Sales, most foreclosure sales are actually auctions. When a property owner has not honored his or her mortgage commitment or agreement, the lender can order the trustee (a third and neutral party between the lender and borrower) to sell the property at a public auction. If you bid at the auction for more than the sum owed on the property, the lender will usually accept your bid. Keep in mind that the mortgage lenders are in the finance business, not the real estate business. They would sooner recover their financial losses (get the money back so that they can lend it out again) than hold out for a profit on the real estate.

THERE ARE WINNERS AND LOSERS AT THE FORECLOSURE SALES

If you buy from the owner before the sale or auction, the owner benefits. Although this sum will probably be less than the full market value of the property, it will be more than he or she would get at the auction because the lender will accept whatever bid will give the lender the most money. In order to get rid of the property, the lender may even accept whatever bid will give the lender the most money. In order to get rid of the property, the owner may even accept a bid that does not cover the entire amount outstanding on the loan, having decided that he can write off at least part of it as a bad debt. However, the lender will subtract from the purchase price not only the loan, but also interest and penalties. Only then would any of the proceeds accrue to the owner. Your offer benefits the owner directly. Because the seller stands to gain little or nothing from a Trustee Sale. You are not taking advantage of him or her.

SAVING MONEY AT THE FORECLOSURE SALE

Foreclosure sales (Trustee Sales) can save you money. A knowledge or property values is especially important. Properties are sold at discounts from the retail market. But the properties are also sold on as "as is" basis. The 30 percent to 50 percent you may have saved could easily be spent on repairing a deteriorating roof, crumbling foundation, or termite damage before you can re-sell the property.

BIDDING PRICE

Keep in mind you will have holding costs, fix-up and rehabilitation costs, and selling costs before you can recover your investment. Add up all your costs before you bid plus your profit.

BUYING BEFORE OR AFTER THE FORECLOSURE SALE

The properties and the circumstances will be different for every sale. If you are buying before the Trustee Sale, you will be able to visit, inspect, and evaluate the property first. If you are buying at the auction, you will not become involved with the emotions of the sellers, you will need few or no negotiation skills.

AUCTION SALES REQUIRE CASH

Most trustees will require that the bidders qualify; you must show your cash or the equivalent up to the amount you intend to bid usually in the form of cashier's checks.

GETTING RICH BUYING FORECLOSURES

Like most of the other ways to make a great deal of money, it takes work and talent, education, and a little luck. You need knowledge, dedication, and perseverance. The profitability is up to you. You can control your destiny through your own efforts.

START MAKING MONEY

This depends on your own motivation and desire. Many people make money after less than one month.

BEGIN PART-TIME

This is probably the best way. While you go through the learning process, you can keep your regular job and build up a reserve of funds to use as fixer-upper or purchase money.

Bidding At Trustee Sales

In your search for the bargain purchases, attend at least four or five actual auctions.

There are several reasons for attending an actual auction:

1. You have plenty of cash and want a bargain property.

2. The current debt is too high and if purchased before the auction there wouldn't be any profit potential. For example, after the auction, the second is extinguished.

3. The seller won't sell before the auction…doesn't make sense but it happens every day.

4. The seller has disappeared and can't be located.

Auctions present opportunities. Here are some of the things you can expect:

1. The auction is relatively quick. Don't be late or you'll miss your chance to bid.

2. Many more people will attend than bid. Expect to see small groups but most of them are spectators. Expect the trustee to verify everyone's qualifications before the auction. Most trustees will request identification and a certified check or cash up to the amount you intend to bid.

3. Know what you are buying! Don't bid on a second mortgage without knowing exactly what is due on the first. Don't forget about taxes and other liens that may have a superior position to the lien which you are bidding on. Research the title and the encumbrances or don't be a player.

4. If you are the high bidder on a second, you can take over the first loan.

Expect one of four events to occur at the Trustee Sale:

1. The sale is postponed (this happens more often than not).

2. The bank is high bidder and gets the property back.

3. A private investor/purchaser like yourself is the high bidder and ends up with the bargain purchase.

4. No one bids and the property goes back to the foreclosing lender.

ISSUES THAT CAN ARISE

If the homeowner is still in the house and you're the successful bidder at the Trustee Sale it will be your responsibility to remove the occupant. You are responsible from the date of the sale for principal, interest, taxes, and insurance payments.

Rules of the Trustee Sale differ from state to state. In some states, cash is needed the day of the auction and it varies from 10 percent to 100 percent of the sale price. For example, in some states if you bid and win, then change your mind after placing a deposit, you can forfeit your deposit and be held liable.

WHAT TO DO BEFORE ATTENDING A TRUSTEE SALE

Verify before attending the auction:

1. Sale/Auction has not been postponed

2. Cash deposit requirements

3. Cash required when it is due

4. Type of payment required: cashier's check, certified check, or money order

5. Don't make the check payable to an institution, make it payable to yourself. Then you can endorse it over to the auctioneer. Otherwise, you may not be able to cash the checks or put them back in your account since they are made payable to an outsider.

Steps before the Trustee Sale

1. Determine market value using comparables, appraisals, and computer sources.

2. Establish your maximum bid and stick with it. Some bidders get caught up in the excitement and forget the objective is not to win the bidding but to get a good deal.

   Last minute cancellations occur quite frequently. Telephone on the day of the auction to verify time, place, and minimum bid. The auctions are frequently cancelled or postponed because the sellers file for bankruptcy to prevent or delay the sale. Another reason for postponement could be that an investor such as yourself has put up the money to stop the foreclosure.

3. At the auction, qualify the other bidders. Only qualified bidders, with certified funds, are supposed to bid. If the Trustee doesn't qualify the bidders you could be bidding against yourself because the other party does not have any money.

What are your intentions for the property? Fix-up, sell in the retail market, or a quick turn-around?

What will you do if the property is auctioned at the sale to the lender? You could write a letter and tell them you observed the Trustee Sale and you want an appointment to discuss the possible purchase of the property. At this point, the property is a REO, and will end up on the new persons desk. He won't even know that he was the high bidder, since the paper work will take days or maybe even weeks to reach him or her. You might end up with a Realtor at this point or possibly the institutional lender will have a staff member handle the situation.

Power of sale foreclosure is used primarily in the western and southern states. The law in these states allows the borrower to waive the right to a court proceeding in the event of a default. This waiver or provision is included in the language of the security instrument (loan document). The instrument's language must specify the notice period and terms under which the foreclosure sale may occur. Each state's status provides for a minimum period of notice to prevent abuses by the lenders.

In most *power of sale* states, the most common security instrument (loan document) is a deed of trust/trust deed. The trust deed is a three-party instrument. The parties involved include the Trustor (borrower), the Trustee (independent third party), and the Beneficiary (lender). The Trustee holds title to the property for the benefit of the Trustor borrower. This right to hold title is granted to the Trustee in the language of the trust deed. The trustee also hold the title to the property for the benefit of the beneficiary. The trustee's only legal rights are to act as a fiduciary and only execute the responsibility that is granted in the trust deed instrument.

If the Trustor borrower defaults, the Trustee is given the right to serve notice in the required manner to the Trustor. This is usually at the request of the lender and was authorized by the signing of the trust deed by the Trustor at the time of the initial borrowing. The notice is in a legal form which is published in the newspaper. The state statutes will allow for the exact details of publication and exposure to the public auction. California is a trustee state.

Power of sale foreclosure, in most cases, is faster and less expensive than other methods of foreclosure. Although there are cases where a lender may want to foreclose via the judicial method. An example of a judicial foreclosure would be if a deficiency judgment is desirable and not obtainable under the power of sale method.

Trustee Sales

An initial step should be an inspection of the property to determine if it is rented, vacant, leased or owner-occupied. The condition and location should be noted to determine if the property is desirable and will serve the purposes of the prospective purchaser.

An appraisal of the market value is necessary in order to form a basis for bidding. Professional appraisers can be employed, tax assessment rolls reviewed, or in some cases, a lender may make an appraisal in connection with a commitment to refinance the property after foreclosure. Some buyers rely on the total amounts shown on the face value of outstanding trust deeds of records. This practice however, does not always present a completely accurate picture.

There always exists the possibility of unpaid balances on prior liens, trust deeds, improvement bonds or delinquent taxes which can cloud title to the property. A preliminary title report can be obtained for a nominal fee from title insurance firms. The report will show unpaid taxes and bonds, and encumbrances such as trust deeds, mortgages and other liens of record. Also, the title report will reveal if a bankruptcy or legal action is pending which can affect title to the property. The possibility of a purchaser to pay prior claims that would remain against the property after the sale should be carefully considered.

When a second or junior trust deed is being foreclosed, a prospective buyer should carefully examine the terms and conditions contained in prior trust deeds of record. Certain clauses are often set forth which would render a new owner liable to make special payments, pay points or additional interest rates, or even cause immediate foreclosure of earlier liens.

A foreclosure sale cannot be made if the owner is in bankruptcy without an order from the bankruptcy court, unless the property has been declared exempt by court order.

Pending foreclosure sales are announced not less than 20 days prior to the time of sale. During the 20-day period the trustor in most cases still has right of redemption; however, the entire amount of all obligations including principal interest, advances and other expenses must be paid.

The trustee gives notice of foreclosure by posting a copy of Notice of Trustee's Sale on the property. A copy of the notice must also be posted in a public place, copies sent to all interested parties and recorded with the county recorder. To assure broadest exposure and availability of a distressed property, publication of the notice must appear once-a-week for three consecutive weeks in a qualified newspaper of general circulation located in the same city (or judicial) district when not located within a city) wherein the subject property is situated. The Daily Commerce is qualified to advertise notices of this type.

Considerable variance is exercised by trustees in preparing sale notices. However, all notices must state the date, time and place of sale; the date and document number under which the trust deed was recorded; the situs if known; name of trustee; and, a legal description of the property being foreclosed. Some trustees will publish the names of trustor, beneficiary and give monetary considerations. Sometimes a limited reference is given to information stated on the previously recorded notice of default.

As required by law, a sales notice will state that payment is to be made in cash "payable at the time of sale in lawful money of the United States." Personal checks are almost never acceptable, at the discretion of the trustee or his sales officer; payment can often be made with a certified or cashier's check from a bank.

The trustee or sales officer will often require bidders to qualify for the sale by requiring a show of funds in advance of the auction. Trustee sales are made "without covenant or warranty, express or implied, regarding title, possession or encumbrances…" Sales are final and the trustee sells only what he holds – the right, title and interest acquired under the deed of trust deposited by the beneficiary with the trustee.

On the date and at the time of sale recited on the sale notice, the trustee will sell the property at public auction to the highest bidder. The first bid is made by the original lender (beneficiary.) The bid is normally an amount equal to the unpaid principal or remainder of the loan, plus accrued interest, advances for taxes and prior encumbrances, insurance and foreclosure costs. Prospective bidders can often, by applying and referring to the trustee's file number stated on the sale notice, obtain advance information concerning the amount of the beneficiary's bid.

The property will go to the beneficiary if no overbids are made at the auction sale. When the property is sold at a higher bid than that made by the beneficiary, the amount due the beneficiary will be paid, the balance goes toward other liens and any excess will be paid to the former owner.

After the sale is made to a successful bidder and the trustee is paid the amount owed, the trustee delivers a trustee's deed to the purchaser. No escrow is necessary. After a three-day notice, a new owner may remove anyone remaining in possession of the property, unless there are prior rights to the deed of trust.

Real Estate Owned (REO)

"Destiny is no matter of chance.
It is a matter of choice.
It is not a thing to be waited for;
it is a thing to be achieved."

—William Jennings Bryan

Real Estate Owned (REO)

Lender-Owned Property

Real Estate Owned (REO) is the real estate used as collateral for loans that have foreclosed. The ownership of the property itself has reverted to the bank, insurance company, or individual lender.

1. **A property becomes a REO when**
   a. Foreclosure process, trough trustee sales (nobody bids)
   b. Deed given to lender in lieu of foreclosure by trustor

2. **How REOs occur**
   a. Refinances
   b. Over-encumbered properties
   c. Private party loans
   d. Payment Shock (ARMS)
   e. Low down payments
   f. Divorce
   g. Non owner occupied loans
   h. Balloon payments
   i. Fraud – Loan qualification and appraisal
   j. Loss of employment (#1 Reason)

REOs have advantages and disadvantages for the foreclosure buyers. The big advantage in buying an REO from the bank is that the lender has the ability to restructure the loan with favorable terms, lower interest rates, and long payment schedules. It is also possible to negotiate and bargain for a waiver of points and fees. There is a good possibility that the lender will even offer a discounted purchase price. But none of these advantages are guaranteed.

The disadvantage is that if no member of the public bids at the Trustee's Sale, the lender may have lent too much on the property or the property might be losing value for some other reason.

3. Advantages in purchasing REO property
   a. Dealing with a non-owner occupant (No personal emotions involved)
   b. Trustee sales wipes out subordinated liens and encumbrances (junior liens are extinguished)
   c. Back taxes paid by beneficiary
   d. If property is vacant, move-in time can be fast

4. Lender disadvantages of owning REO property
   a. Possibility of doing an eviction of the previous owner
   b. Vacancy; vandalism and fire insurance
   c. Property taxes
   d. Insurance payments and or homeowner association dues
   e. Monthly mortgage payments on any senior liens and encumbrances
   f. Deferred maintenance –– fix up costs
   g. Maintenance cost while holding property (Landscaping and pool)
   h. Opportunity cost REO is a non-performing asset, and are carried as assets.

The foreclosure action is a result of a borrower's defaulting on a loan that was secured by real estate. Usually, a lender has lent money to the owner of a property and the property is used as security to assure the lender that the loan will be repaid. If the lender does not receive payments as promised and agreed, the lender has the authority, given when the borrower signs the trust deed or mortgage, to foreclosure under the contract. In California, the buyer signs a deed of trust and a promissory note. In other states, the relevant document may be called a mortgage and promissory note.

The deed of trust (mortgage) contains a provision that requires the beneficiary (the lender) to deliver the note and deed of trust to an independent third party called a Trustee. The Trustee holds the deed of trust and note until it is paid in full. If the property owner does not pay as agreed, the beneficiary (lender) will advise the Trustee (the third party) to sell the property to the highest bidder at a Trustee's Sale and then repay the loan with the proceeds from the sale. The Trustee will advertise the property for sale in a legal newspaper and possibility in other papers of general circulation.

If the Trustee announces the auction (Trustee Sale) to sell the property and no one show up to make a competitive bid, the lender automatically bids for the property at the minimum price that the announcement advertised as the sale price. In common terms, that is referred to as "the lender bids in." The astute buyer contacts the lender after the sale and starts negotiations. If the lender is foreclosing on a property with more equity than the mortgage value, for example, a $200,000 mortgage and a $300,000 sale value. The lender knows that this type of sale will attract a crowd to the Trustee's Sale. In other circumstances, the lender will be motivated to sell the property. However, being motivated does not mean that the lender will give you the property. The bank officer you talk with will be obligated to sell for the highest price possible. After all, he works for the bank, and stockholders really frown on his giving money away.

5. **REO Sources (potentially anyone who creates or services a loan bank)**
   a. Banks
   b. Savings and Loan Associations
   c. Thrifty and Loan
   d. Mortgage Bankers
   e. FDIC   Bank failures
   f. FSLIC   Saving and loan failures
   g. FHA   Largest REO holder in USA
   h. VA   Largest single family resident REO holder in the US
   i. PMI   Private mortgage insurance companies
   j. Small Mortgage Companies

6. **Locating lenders owning repossessed property**
   a. Newspaper classified section for VA and FHA financed HUD listings
   b. Track default notices (Hot Sheets) geographic area targeted
   c. Yellow Pages; look under Banks, Savings and Loan Associations, Thrift and Loans. You will find yourself making a lot of phone calls, this is a difficult method and not recommended.

7. **Which lenders are best to work with?**
   a. Institution assets vs liabilities; how much of a lenders reserve capital is locked up in non-performing assets (REOs), FDIC and FSLIC reserve requirements, at some point, a lender will be forced to liquidate their non-performing assets.
   b. Reasons for large REO inventories
      1. Overly aggressive lending policies
      2. Bad appraisals
      3. Types of loans used (negative amortization or high caps)
      4. Low down payments - FHA and VA
      5. Refinance and run
      6. Changes in interest rates, economy, tax laws

  c. Does the lender automatically list property with a Realtor?
    1. Seller pays the fees on commission, do not let this stop you, it is not a disadvantage. Common with large S & Ls and banks after several weeks of processing. If listed, deal with the listing agent and not the lender.

Expect no favors and don't believe everything you read in the newspapers about financial institutions going broke and just crying to rid themselves of REO. You approach the lender with a win-win attitude, you'll open the door. REOs can be a gold mine, but like all mining, will take some effort and time. Remember: Bank officers are being evaluated by their superiors every day, not to mention by the bank board and the FDIC. In the negotiations, you therefore become a real opponent. Work at building rapport and a long-term relationship will develop.

None of these lenders is in the real estate business. Their business is in the lending of money, and every property that finds its way back to them as an REO is a mark of an unsuccessful deal. Therefore, these lenders are motivated sellers. Motivated sellers are what you need to make a success of the distressed property business.

Banks and savings and loan associations have special rules about the disposition (sale) of REOs. For example, they almost always get an appraisal; they usually ask a broker or professional contractor to estimate the fix-up costs, and they usually attempt to sell the property themselves or to deal with a local broker.

If you plan to purchase from the bank or institution, you must know the value of the property before you contact the bank for an appointment. It is wise also to attend the sale to find out what price the institution paid to get the property back. With these two pieces of information you will know what you can pay and what openings there are for bargaining and negotiation. Sellers will always listen to proposals that either make their position better or eliminate risk of future loss.

If your initial telephone call does not reach the correct person at the bank, you will end up frustrated because the business of REO and foreclosure is usually one of the least advertised, least-known departments in the bank. Be sure you get the proper department.

Even if you do get the right department, your initial telephone call may be surprising; you may be told that the bank has no REOs. Of course, you've already been to the Trustee's Sale and know that it does. That answer may be prompted by one of two reasons. The REO department may not have had the property turned over to it as of yet, or if you are telephoning out of the blue, the bank will not know that you are not a stockholder checking to see if it has made any bad loans. Banks and savings and loan associations tend to be pretty closed about REOs, justifiably, since REOs depress their earnings. What you must do, having discovered the property identity, is to visit the institution yourself and talk to the REO department.

   A few weeks later follow up with another letter. Send a series of at least three. Then begin to call on the REO department regularly. Request meetings with the REO officer or officers and tell them what you can do for them.

8. Presentation
   a. Find the decision maker.
   b. Ability to qualify for loan and have money for a down payment
       With a large down payment of 20% - 25%, or more, non-qualifying loans are available and private mortgage insurance. (PMI) can be avoided.
   c. The deposit should be what is asked for by the lender or 3% of the purchase price. This will become part of your down payment and a copy of a personal check submitted with your offer is common.
   d. None of the following should be in your offer: Promissory Notes, using a assignee or nominee buyer, assuming the loan (if it's a "1st" there is no loan to assume). Down payment cannot be borrowed money. Multiple credit cards don't work. Lender will verify income source.
   e. Useful questions to ask when writing offers:
       1. Is the lender selling for under "Book In Value"? (Amount of loan balance when property went to Trustee Sale)
       2. Are you selling for under "Book In Value"? Will the lender take a loss?
       4. How to find "Book In Value". Ask the customer service representative of a title company to give you the amount the property went to Trustee Sale for on the "Trustees Deed".
       5. Is in-house financing made available?
       6. Does in-house financing make the price lower?
       7. Will buyer financing make price lower?
       8. How fast can the lender close escrow?
       9. What escrow and title companies does the lender use?
       10. What forms of prequalification are required as proof to be submitted with tax returns etc.?
       11. Is a specific type of purchase contract needed to submit an offer on? (Example: California Association of Realtors, or CAR form)

9. Viewing the property

a. Responsibility: Leave exactly as found! This includes keys, lock boxes, lights, doors, windows, gates, and appliances.

b. Always knock before entering any house.

c. Do not rely on lender's inspection. Fix-up costs must be determined. I recommend a professional home inspection if you are genuinely interested in buying the property. Inspection clauses in a purchase contract are a loophole to lower your offer after an inspection Write inspection clauses into all of your offers. There are many home inspection services to choose from.
Example of a home inspection clause that can be used when writing an offer. This offer is subject to buyer's reasonable approval, at buyer's expense, of a home inspection of the property. If escrow holder receives no written disapproval from buyer within _____ business days after sellers acceptance hereof, this contingency will be deemed approved.

d. Look around the area. Write down "For Sale", "For Rent", and "Sold" signs. These may be used as comparables for determining market value. Talk to the people you see. Sometimes you find out important information. A good way of meeting people in an area is by knocking on doors of neighbors and garage sales.

e. If the property has a Homeowner's Association, a financial statement of the Homeowner's Association must be reviewed, this should include the percentage of owner occupied units, and the monthly fees.

f. Ordering a Property Profile from a title company. Obtain a profile with comps included. A title company will only deliver to a business address; but, you can stop by and pick up profiles at the title company. Make sure you give them back your business.

10. Submitting an offer

a. Use a Real Estate Purchase Contract and Receipt for Deposit. Some lenders in California require an offer to be written on a C.A.R. Form.

b. When referring to property, lenders use either property address, trustee sale number, or name of foreclosed owner (property address is generally used.)

c. California Law on Sellers Disclosure Statement Lenders are exempt from providing a buyer with a Sellers Disclosure Statement when selling REO property. (Lender has never lived in property.

d. Submit a copy of a personal check or cashiers check for the deposit with offer.

e. Buy "As Is" and do fix-up work yourself. Most lenders will not provide a termite report and this may have to be provided for by the buyer.

f. Assume any senior liens, no subject-to's if taking over an existing loan.

g. Find out if lender wants to do their own financing. Ask for an accommodation loan on REO property, generally 1-1 ?% less than the going rate for fixed interest and many times 10% down and no PMI.

h. Provide information to back up and support your offer.

   1. Comps (properties that are similar and have recently sold)
   2. Professional estimates of deferred maintenance (home inspection services)
   3. Take photographs to educate REO officer/committee.

11. Final strategies

a. Provide dual offers giving lender an option.

b. Offers prior to trustee sale – no paperwork/appraisal.

c. Cash speaks louder than financing. (plus Short Escrows)

Short Pay Sales

*"Shoot for the moon.
Even if you miss it, you will
land among the stars."*

—Les Brown

Short Pay Sales

As the number of borrowers falling behind on their mortgage payments climbs to the highest level in five years, the number of "short sales" is increasing.

In a short sale of a home, a lender allows the property to be sold for less than the total amount due. In many cases, the lender forgives the remaining debt.

Economist attribute the increase in delinquencies in part to a weaker housing market and the widespread use of adjustable-rate mortgages, many of which now are resetting at higher rates. In addition, as demand for mortgages softened, lenders loosened their standards and made riskier loans.

For a lender, a short sale can be appealing because the process can be shorter and less costly than foreclosing, especially in a declining market. Lender can avoid the cost of property maintenance, utilities and homeowners' association fees.

For borrowers, a short sale is a way to avoid having a foreclosure on their credit report. A short sale can be less of a black mark than a foreclosure on a borrower's credit record because it indicates that the borrower was working with the lender.

Under certain circumstances, the debt forgiven by the bank may be taxable to the borrower. Borrowers who have a mortgage and a home-equity loan may also have to negotiate with two lenders or two departments of the same bank.

Original Mortgage Or Refinanced Mortgage

When funds are borrowed to buy a home, it is considered a "purchase-money" loan. That makes it a non-recourse loan under California law. If a borrower owes $300,000 on a home that's now worth only $200,000 the most the lender can do is take over the home. The lender cannot sue to get the difference from the borrower.

Many homeowners have refinanced due to the drop in mortgage rates in the past year. Most refis are recourse loans, the lender has the right to seek a deficiency judgment in court against a borrower if the foreclosed property is worth less than the debt still owed by the borrower. The lender could judicially foreclose on a house and seek an additional deficiency judgment from the homeowner. However, this method has rarely been employed by lenders because it can take more than a year.

The more common way is what's known as a non-judicial foreclosure, a lender directs a trustee to foreclose according to the lender's rights under the loan note and the deed of trust.

The internal revenue service treats the foreclosure like a sale of property for the debt. There is tax to be paid if the tax basis of the property is lower than the sale price. A homeowner could owe the IRS money even if their home is worth less than the sale price.

When a loan is a recourse debt (a refinanced loan), the IRS will seek it's share of any cancellation indebtedness. This tax can be avoided, if the debtor is insolvent or in bankruptcy. The lender will probably threaten a judicial foreclosure that they can get a deficiency judgment. Most lenders will not follow through on such a threat, because of the time involved. A judicial foreclosure takes much longer than a non-judicial foreclosure; the borrower also gets a right of redemption. That means that the borrower has a year because the title is clouded.

In a non-judicial foreclosure there is a trustee sale on the 111th day conducted by the trustee if the sale brings in more than the amount owed on the note, this money is transferred from the trustee to the trustor (borrower). If there's a deficiency, California law prohibits the lender in a non-judicial foreclosure from going after the borrower for the balance.

Short Pay

Some home owners are "up side down" Their existing loan balance(s) and other liens exceed the price they can get for their property. Therefore, the only way they can sell, without going through foreclosure or bankruptcy; is to add cash to the escrow or get their lender(s) to agree to a short pay off. A short pay off is where the lender agrees to accept less than the outstanding balance as payment for the debt.

The lender will require a good reason to sell now, instead of waiting until the market recovers.

A lender may consider a short pay off if the reason for the sale is due to:

1. Unemployment
2. Divorce
3. Too many debts
4. Illness
5. Death
6. Relocation

A short sale allows the owners to sell their property at current market prices, turn the proceeds over to the lender, and perhaps survive with their credit intact or moderately damaged.

A short sale is strictly between the old owner and their lender. The new buyer can go to any lender. The title will show no trace of the former owner's financial problem.

Sellers who win a short sale agreement from their lenders should consult a tax advisor. A short sale may drive up a seller's tax liability.

What if the seller files bankruptcy or is already in bankruptcy?

Once the court determines that the property is over encumbered and there is no equity to pay other creditors, the property will eventually be removed from bankruptcy protection, and the lender will continue with the foreclosure. The "cram down" technique has been rejected by the courts for owner occupied 1-4 units, but not for commercial, industrial, and apartments. Refer the seller to an attorney if the issue of bankruptcy arises.

Short Pay-Off Agreement

You need to make your offer contingent upon getting an agreement for a short pay off from the lender(s). The following should be in the purchase contract:

1. The offer is contingent upon the seller's ability to obtain a short pay off agreement from the lender.

2. Due to the need to obtain a short pay off agreement from the lender, the closing could take longer than normal.

3. A notice of default should be noted in the deposit receipt if filed by the lender.

A signed offer is when you approach the lender about a short pay off.

1. The request must come from the seller in the form of a hardship letter.

2. Submit a copy of the buyer's offer, with the seller's acceptance contingent upon the lender's approval. Attach documents showing the buyer's ability to purchase.

3. Submit a rough estimate of the amount of short pay off it will take to close escrow.

4. Attach photos and comp sales.

Ask the lender(s) if they have a specific checklist when bringing in the offer.

Your offer to the lender(s) should be mailed by Federal Express and followed up with a phone call.

During the escrow period, keep in touch with the lender.

Lender Package

The following items should be contained in your package to the lender, unless the lender has provided you with a specific checklist.

1. Cover letter from you.

2. Sellers letter giving you permission to talk to the lender.

3. Short pay off letter from the seller outlining reason(s) for short pay off.

4. Purchase contact signed by seller(s) and buyer(s).

5. Acknowledgement that the seller(s) will receive no proceeds in the transaction.

6. Certified copy of escrow instructions.

7. Preliminary title report.

8. Comps in the area.

9. Financial qualifications of the buyer(s).

10. A letter to the lender pointing out their acquisition costs, including trust deed sale, property management fees, maintenance fees, insurance costs, association fees, taxes, eviction costs and marketing expenses.

11. You will help discourage the seller's removal of items such as appliances, window coverings, plants and attached vandalism.

12. The property is not vacant, thus not subject to vandalism.

You are requesting the sellers not to file bankruptcy which could delay the lenders process in acquiring the property from 4 months to a year.

Federal Express the package to the lender and follow up with a phone call.

Disclosure In The Listing Agreement And MLS

All potential buyers should be informed of the over encumbered situation. To give the disclosure you must get the seller's release in writing in the listing agreement. Things to include as part of the listing agreement:

1. Seller authorizes broker to inform buyers and other brokers of the need to obtain agreement from the lender(s) to accept a less than full pay off to enable the sale close at the listing price.

2. Seller agrees to the commission per the contract even though the seller may not receive cash from the sale.

3. Seller agrees to allow submission to MLS stating that the sale terms are "subject to consent of the lender(s)... contact listing agent for details".

4. Seller agrees to allow the broker to contact lender(s) to discuss the problem and seller agrees to sign a letter authorizing the lender to accept the broker as the seller's representative (most lenders will not negotiate with a broker without this letter of authorization).

5. Seller understands that there are income tax ramifications when a property is sold on a short pay off. Seller is instructed to seek a competent tax person and that the broker is not giving tax advice nor liable for any income tax consequences.

When debt is forgiven, lenders must, as of 1/1/94, send the IRS a 1099 form. In some cases this can trigger ordinary income of the debt forgiveness and/ or a capital gain on the sale. There are some bankruptcy and insolvency rules that can defeat debt forgiveness as income, but this should be referred to an attorney or tax specialist.

6. Seller understands that many lenders have various "workout programs" that may allow the seller to keep the home, even though the seller still wishes to list the home for sale with the broker.

What Are The Benefits of a Short Pay-Off To All The Parties?

Borrower

- Lower the debt enough to sell the property
- Can avoid foreclosure

Lender or Current Investor Holding The Note

- Avoids another REO
- Saves money by avoiding foreclosure, holding, and resale costs

PMI Insurer

- Avoids another REO

Listing An Over Encumbered Property

1. Determine the listing price using market comps, do not add up the loan balances + closing cost and call that the listing price. Remember properties sell based on market value, not seller's obligations.

2. Estimate the total dollar amount it will take to close the escrow outstanding loan balances + late fees + seller's complete closing cost + any personal judgments and tax liens + withholding requirements for foreign or out of state sellers.

3. The difference between #1 and #2 is your short fall

   Listing/Sales Price (based on market comps)
   - less encumbrances, liens, personal judgments
   - less seller closing cost (including your commission)
   - less taxes withheld for foreigners/out of state seller
   ───
   = Amount Short from Sale that needs to be negotiated

NOTE: If there is an IRS lien on the property before the property can be sold, a CERTIFICATION OF DISCHARGE OF PROPERTY FROM FEDERAL LIEN *must be obtained from the IRS.*

Approach The Lender Before You Receive An Offer

1. Find out who handles short pay-off's… the person can be called a "work out specialist" or "short payoff department" or some other name. If you wait until you have a buyer in escrow, it could take too long and your buyer could get discouraged and drop out.

2. A lender usually will not consider anything until you have a qualified buyer with a specific offer. But you need to know in advance who to talk to, what are the steps, and what is the required paperwork. Ask if the lender has a short pay off check sheet, listing the items that the lender requires.

3. If there is a second Deed of Trust ahead of the upside down first loan, this can be the "deal killer." Many first loan holders refuse to allow a holder of a second to get any money. But a broker must talk a holder of a second into signing a Deed of Reconveyance to free up the title for the new buyer's lender.

4. Each lender has their own list of requirements, but most want:

   a. Statement of the borrower/seller's financial condition, including tax returns, balance sheets, and profit and loss statements. If the borrower has lots of other assets and money, the lender may require the borrower to add some cash as a condition of accepting short pay off amount.

   b. Signed statement that the seller is receiving no money of any sort from the sale. An agent who "kickbacks" a part of the commission to the borrower/seller is committing fraud and if caught will have severe legal problems.

   c. Plus the following:
      1. Copy of the new buyer's offer
      2. Certified copy of the escrow instruction for the resale
      3. Estimate closing statement by the escrow officer
      4. Copy of the preliminary title report
      5. Copy of the new buyer's loan approval, or loan application if not yet approved

Laws

"The way I see it, if you want the rainbow, you gotta put up with the rain."

—Dolly Parton

Laws
(As they apply to the purchase of homes in foreclosure)

During previous periods of hard times and the resulting large numbers of foreclosures, many unfortunate property owners were duped into losing their homes through the foreclosure process.

Once they became behind in their payments, they were contacted by a person who offered to assist them in their time of need. This "Mortgage Foreclosure Consultant", who promised to help the homeowner save his home, graciously took his fee in advance, generally in the form of a note which was a lien on the property.

The homeowners thought that their problems were being solved for them, and they did nothing more about solving their problem themselves. After all, they had just hired a professional to help them through their temporary difficulty.

Unfortunately, their paid consultant did nothing either. The one thing that the consultant DID do was to foreclose on the note he took back as his fee for helping the homeowner, and helped himself to the homeowner's property.

That is why many states wrote laws to protect homeowners who were facing foreclosure, in an effort to protect them from lying predators who offered assistance and ended up with the property.

Laws Vary From State To State

Although the investment principles and the ideas that I included in this book work in most areas of the country, it is important to check carefully the local laws. While many laws are very similar in nature and purpose, it is impossible in a book of this kind to interpret the real estate laws for all fifty states and set down one group of rules for all of them. For instance, some states have mortgages; other states have Deeds of Trust. Some states have second and third Deeds of Trusts while others have second or third mortgages. Even if the terms can be often interchanged and there might be little difference between the two, it is better to consult a trusted attorney or accountant to get a specific question answered concerning a specific area It is not the purpose of this book to give legal or tax service.

Supreme Court Upholds Constitutionality Of Foreclosure Procedure

In November of 1978, by a vote of seven to two, the Supreme Court upheld the procedure under which the California and other mortgage lenders can foreclose on a home without first giving the homeowner a chance for a hearing. Due to a century-old California law, a creditor can foreclose on a home by sending out a Notice of Default informing the owner that he has three months to pay the money allegedly due. After that period has passed the property can be auctioned. Approximately half of the states have similar procedures permitting foreclosure without a court hearing. This means heavier pressure will be exerted by the lenders to recover and force the sale of the property thereby probably wiping out all equity of the original borrower. This also means, there will be an increasing opportunity, of alerting real estate specialists to help themselves and the troubled owner.

Although acquiring single family homes and other properties in this manner has been done for the past twenty to thirty years, with the law changes and the economic environment of the country, it is a totally new ball game offering new opportunities in favor of the individual small investor.

Some Examples Of California Foreclosure Laws

HUD LAWS

FHA has first right to take over payments on its loans. If the Trustor does not qualify; foreclosure can proceed.
FHA can extend credit to the Trustor.
VA will also give extensions.

AB 510

Forbids unconscionable mechanics contracts.
Trustor can void title change if it occurs within the 45 days of the default.
No selling or factoring of notes (no assignment).
Courts will define unconscionable.

AB 610

Makes contracts easier for borrower to understand.
Most put in bold type the following: IF YOU SIGN THIS CONTRACT, YOU PUT YOUR HOME UP FOR POSSIBLE SALE IF YOU DEFAULT.

AB 827

Revised the default notice publications to be clearer than previously; adds more information.
Unconscionable contracts are automatically void.
Trustor has two years to contest an unconscionable act.

SB 1126

Does everything AB 510 does, plus the following:
Trustee cannot have an interest in the property.
Grants power of postponements of sale.
Beneficiary has power to postpone sale up to three times. Further postponing of the sale reactivates the reinstatement period.

SB 1128

Laws regarding foreclosure consultants; standardizes the contract form.
Cannot change title for 6 days.
Cannot record title for 6 days.
Cannot transfer any interest for 6 days.
No monetary exchange for 6 days.
No false appraisal statements. (punishable by an amount equal to three times equity)
Foreclosure contract must be written in property owner's language.
(Check your state for Foreclosure Laws)

History Of The "Double Whammy"

In November 1985, the Federal Home Loan Bank Board (FHLBB) issued a new generation prohibiting the practice of some lenders who call a loan due when a property is sold and charge a prepayment penalty (called the "double whammy"). Although a prior FHLBB regulation held that a due-on-sale clause could not be enforced when a prepayment penalty was charged, many lenders took the position that this prohibition only applied after a "subject to" property transfer-where the lender subsequently called the loan due on sale.

The FHLBB regulations clear up this confusion. For loans secured by owner-occupied, one-to-four family residential property, the double whammy prohibition also applies for a period of time after the lender fails to allow a qualified transferee to assume the loan at its current rate and terms.

The Lenders "Double Whammy"

The Double Whammy is an informal, "non-legal" term, that means the attempt by a lender to charge a prepayment penalty when a loan is paid off, before its scheduled maturity date, because of the lender's demand for payment when a sale of transfer for the property occurs. In other words, it is an attempt to simultaneously enforce both a due-on-sale clause and a prepayment penalty clause in a note, deed of trust, or other loan documents.

The Federal Home Loan Bank Board has curtailed mortgage lenders' rights to impose pre-payment penalties on homeowners seeking to transfer their loan to new buyers.

If you own a home and have a Deed of Trust from a local savings & loan association that has a "due on sale" clause, the clause permits the lender to demand full payment of your loan, or raise the interest rate if you sell or transfer title. This clause effectively prevents you from passing on your low-interest loan to a new buyer.

Your loan documents may have a prepayment penalty in the small print. This permits the lender to charge a substantial sum if you pay off the loan early.

Here comes the "Double Whammy". The lender warns you that any transfer of your loan will trigger a foreclosure action based upon the due-on-sale provisions of your loan. If you sell the house without the loan attached and prepay the loan, the lender then will impose a prepayment penalty.

The bottom line is this; if a mortgage lender imposes a prepayment penalty, it may not enforce a due-on-sale clause.

SCORE ONE FOR US!

Regulation, Guidelines And Federal Prohibitions

Question: Does the federal law prohibit the "double whammy"?

Answer: Yes. Under the federal regulation, a prepayment penalty imposed by any type of lender is prohibited when a loan is paid off in connection with the sale or transfer or property. More specifically, a prepayment penalty is prohibited when:

1. The lender declares by written notice that the loan is due pursuant to a due-on-sale clause, or

2. The lender begins foreclosure proceedings (either judicial or nonjudicial) to enforce a due-on-sale clause, or

3. The lenders fail to approve a completed credit application of a "qualified transferee" who wishes to assume the loan within 30 days after the lender receives the completed application. There after, the property is transferred to that transferee and the loan is paid off within 120 days after the lender receives the completed application.

Bankruptcy

The common types of bankruptcy actions are Chapter 7 ("Liquidation"), Chapter 11 ("Reorganization"), and Chapter 13 ("Plan of Adjustment", for debtor and regular income). Chapters 7 and 11 may be used by individuals and most types of business entities, including corporations and partnerships. Chapter 13 may be used only by an individual, or by a married couple filling jointly.

HOW LISTINGS ARE AFFECTED BY BANKRUPTCY

If an owner of real property has entered into a listing contract with a broker and then files a petition under Chapter 7, 11, or 13, the listing contract is treated as any other "executory contract" under bankruptcy law. This means that the Bankruptcy Trustee may either affirm or reject the contract, depending on whether the Trustee considers it favorable to the bankruptcy estate. If the contract is affirmed, it will remain in effect on its original terms. If it is rejected, the licensee may file his own creditor's claim for breach of contract, along with the debtor's other unsecured creditors.

The time within which the Trustee must affirm or reject an executory contract depends on the Chapter under which the debtor files. However, it is possible to shorten this time period by filing a complaint or petition with the Bankruptcy Court.

THE AUTHORITY FOR THE BANKRUPTCY LAW

Bankruptcy law is federal law in the United States. It is provided for in the U.S. Constitution, which says that Congress shall have the power to establish "uniform laws on the subject of bankruptcy throughout the United States." The current law on the subject was enacted by Congress as the "Bankruptcy Act of 1978", which can be found in Title 11 of the United States Code.

THE EFFECT OF A BANKRUPTCY ON A PENDING FORECLOSURE

From the moment a petition is filed by a debtor under Chapter 7, 11, or 13, federal law imposes an automatic stay on all civil proceedings against the debtor or the debtor's property. This includes all acts to foreclose a trust deed, mortgage, or other lien on the debtor's property, whether by power of sale of judicial foreclosure.

THE "AUTOMATIC STAY"

The automatic stay applies, regardless of whether the debtor's petition is filed when a secured creditor is about to record a notice of default, or in the middle of the reinstatement period (in a power of sale foreclosure), or one minute before the foreclosure process is complete. In all cases, the automatic stay operates as an injunction to prevent further action by a creditor until permission has been granted by the U.S. Bankruptcy Court.

A SECURED CREDITOR CAN OBTAIN PERMISSION TO PROCEED WITH A FORECLOSURE

A creditor must file a Complaint For Relief From Automatic Stay in the U.S. Bankruptcy Court where the debtor's petition was filed. From the time the creditor files a Complaint for Relief, the process will take a minimum of 30 to 60 days, and may take as much as 120 days or longer.

The first hearing on the complaint must be held within 30 days after the complaint is filed by the creditor At the hearing, the court may grant the creditor relief by terminating the stay, or may continue the hearing for one additional 30-day period, or may otherwise modify or extend the Automatic Stay.

Among the most important issues the court will consider are:

1. Whether the debtor has equity in the property which could be salvaged by allowing the debtor a reasonable period of time to sell the property;

2. Whether the debtor needs the property to effect a reorganization (e.g., where the debtor filed a Chapter 11 Reorganization);

3. Is the creditor adequately protected?

Always check to see if an owner in foreclosure is in Bankruptcy. Once the Bankruptcy is lifted you can then work with the owner.

DEFENSES TO THE SALE

Question: How does bankruptcy protect a trustor?

Answer: Upon filing a bankruptcy petition, the trustor's secured and unsecured creditors may no longer take steps to enforce the trustor's debts. Foreclosure actions already commenced against the trustor must be stayed. A creditor who willfully violates this "Automatic Stay" may be held in contempt of court and may be liable to the bankruptcy estate for damages (including punitive damages).

Question: Are there any exceptions to the Automatic Stay?

Answer: Yes. The beneficiary may obtain relief from the Automatic Stay if he can either, (a) show good cause as to why he should be allowed to enforce his claims against the trustor, or (b) show that the trustor lacks equity in the property and that the property is not necessary to an effective reorganization. While the law clearly does not define "cause" a common cause for seeking relief from the Automatic Stay is a lack of adequate protection for the beneficiary. Actions taken by the trustor in bad faith or for the purpose of stalling a legitimate creditor's claim may also constitute cause for relief from the Automatic Stay.

   To obtain relief from the Automatic Stay, the beneficiary must bring a motion in Bankruptcy Court in accordance with the procedural rules of the United States Bankruptcy Code.

Question: Must the trustee give a new notice of sale after obtaining relief from the automatic stay?

Answer: Yes, generally in most cases.

ENJOINING THE SALE

Question: Under what circumstances may the trustee obtain an injunction against the trustee's sale?

Answer: An injunction may be granted if, (a) there has been no default on the obligation or the amount in default has not been properly computed, (b) a statue of limitations has rendered the debt unenforceable, (c) the creditor's alleged lien does not really exist, or (d) the trustee did not comply with applicable notice requirements.

Question: Who may seek to enjoin the sale?

Answer: Usually the trustor will be the one seeking the injunction. However, junior beneficiaries who would be affected by the sale can usually seek injunctive relief against the foreclosing beneficiary. Senior beneficiaries and former owners of the property generally have no right to enjoin the sale.

Question: What are the procedures for enjoining a trustee's sale?

Answer: The procedures for enjoining a trustee's sale involve complex rules of court procedure and strategic concerns which are beyond the scope of this book. Anyone wishing to enjoin a trustee's sale should contact legal counsel.

"Due On Sale" Clause

A "due on sale" clause guarantees the bank the right to demand all moneys owed it when the property changes hands. The clause was first instituted some decades back because, although interest rates had risen substantially over the years, existing mortgages were being transferred with no approval needed and with interest rates well below the current market. Older mortgages, particularly those that were VA guaranteed or FHA insured, were being transferred to new owners at older, lower rates of interest with no credit check. With a "due on sale" provision, banks could ask for a higher rate and approve the creditworthiness of the new purchaser.

If you can offer the bank the hope of avoiding a foreclosure and commit believably to making all the payments yourself, you will probably be successful.

Banks really do not want to acquire the property, they would much prefer to concentrate on the business of selling or renting money. Once banks are put into the position of being property owners, they share the burdens, problems, and objectives of all the other people who own and want to sell their property.

Remember that although the loan is generally far in excess of the homeowner's equity in the property, the bank really does not own the house until a foreclosure situation develops. At that point, the bank does have to take over things like watering the lawn, cutting the grass, and the hundred and one other chores that homeowners must perform. And that's not really the bank's idea of the ideal job. But when the banker moves into title through the foreclosing process, he owns the property and must see that such work is done.

Many banks have a property management officer who has the responsibility of safeguarding properties. Some banks employ property management concerns, usually local real estate brokers who provide the services for a fee. Of course, that's a fee the bank would rather not have to pay. If the property is damaged through vandalism or natural causes, the banks have to decide what to do in response.

It should be clear that the bank really has no interest in foreclosing on the property. When a bank has to do so, it adds a new obligation to the debit side of the financial statement. That debit is known as real estate owned, often referred to as REO. Bankers hate to have this show up in their statements. REOs represent loans that went sour, even though all the most conservative standards were applied in the consideration of the original application.

Have the "Due On Sale" clause waived by the lender in writing.

Tax Legislation
1997 Tax Relief Act

Current capital gains legislation will now permit you to sell your residence and retain a profit on the sale of up to $500,000 without increasing taxes! You don't even have to buy another home to shelter the profit from capital gains tax! You may choose to buy a less expensive residence and invest the profit elsewhere.

Mechanics' Liens

Those who perform work or furnish material, equipment, or are in the construction or repair of real estate improvements are entitled to file at the county recorder's office a mechanic's lien against the property if their bills are not paid when due.

Those entitled to file mechanic's liens include original contractors, subcontractors, carpenters, plumbers, painters, plasterers, laborers, material suppliers and architects.

An original contractor is one who contracts directly with the owner. A subcontractor contracts for a job with the original contractor.

A mechanic's lien is a special lien, as it creates a lien only against the specific property on which the work is done or materials furnished; other property belonging to the owner is not subject to the lien.

TRUE LIMITS

When a lien claim is recorded, the property stands as security. To create a valid liens the law requires that claimants record their lien claims within certain time limits. All claimants have 90 days from the completion of the project in which to file their claims, provided no Notice of Completion has been filed (recorded) by the owner. If the owner records a Notice of Completion, the time is reduced to 60 days from the date of recordation for original contractors and 30 days for all other claimants. Lien claims must be VERIFIED (sworn to be the truth) to be recorded.

If after recording the liens they remain unpaid, then the claimants, to protect their security, must within 90 days from the date of recordation, file a mechanic's lien foreclosure suit. When the judgment is obtained by the claimants, the court may then order the property sold by the sheriff to satisfy the liens under a procedure similar to a mortgage foreclosure suit. That is to say, the property owner has an equity of redemption for one year from the date of sale.

If the lien foreclosure suit is not filed within 90 days, then the claims become outlawed insofar as holding the property as security. However, the claimants still have a right to file a regular open account suit and obtain an unsecured judgment against those who hired them.

NOTICE OF NON-RESPONSIBILITY

If an owner leases his property and the lessee makes certain repairs or improvements without the knowledge of the owner, the owner's property may be subject to the liens. However, if he discovers the work is being done or materials furnished, he must, within 10 days from the date of such discovery, post a NOTICE OF NON-RESPONSIBILITY on the property if he is to continue to have his property saved from liens. He must also, within the 10-day period, record a copy of the Notice of Non-Responsibility at the county recorder's office. If this is done, then the lien claimants can only hold the leaseholder's interest as security for their liens. Very often with the passing for time and the increase in the rental value of property, leases become quite valuable and a lease is subject to sale the same as any other interest in real estate.

PRIORITY

Ordinarily, a mortgage or trust deed recorded against real estate takes priority over any liens recorded subsequently. The law provides, however, that a mechanic's lien recorded after a mortgage or trust deed will step ahead of those liens if any work is done or material furnished on the property before they are recorded. For instance, when building loans are made, it is usual for the lender to inspect the property to be sure that no work has started or material delivered on the premises before he advances the money. Even though no mechanic's lien rights are then existing, any that may arise later will date back in order of preference to the time the work was first started. This gives all subsequent mechanic's lien holders priority over any mortgages or trust deeds that were not recorded before the work started or material furnished.

PRE-LIEN NOTICE

Since many owners found themselves faced with a mechanic's lien from subcontractors who had not been paid by the general contractor, (even though the owner had paid the general contractor) it is now required that every person who furnishes labor, service, equipment or material for which a mechanic's lien can be claimed, except a person under direct contract with owner or one performing   actual labor for wages, as a necessary prerequisite to the validity of any claim of lien subsequently filed, to give written notice to the owner, the general contractor and the construction lender, if there is one, of their contribution to the work. This must be done within 20 days of first providing their labor, services, equipment or materials to the job.

Rents, Profits, And Possession

Question: May the beneficiary collect rents and profits from the real property security prior to the trustee's sale if the trustor defaults on the obligation?

Answer: Not unless, (a) the deed of trust specifically gives the beneficiary that right with a "rent-and-profits clause" or (b) the beneficiary takes possession of the property.

Question: What procedures should the beneficiary use for collecting rents and profits?

Answer: The beneficiary can ask the trustor to collect the rent and profits on the beneficiary's behalf, or may collect rent directly from tenants (with the trustor's consent), or, if the tenants and/or trustor will not cooperate with the beneficiary, the beneficiary may request the court to appoint a receiver even if the tenants and trustor are cooperative to avoid any possibility of being deemed in possession of the property, and to avoid a violation of the one form of action rule.

Question: May the beneficiary take possession of the property prior to a trustee's sale if the trustor defaults on the obligation?

Answer: Not unless the deed of trust specifically gives the beneficiary that right. A beneficiary who exercises such a right is known as a "mortgage in possession."

Question: What are the advantages and disadvantages of becoming a "mortgage in possession"?

Answer: The advantages include the following:
- Since the trustor facing foreclosure would not be motivated to care for the property properly, the beneficiary can protect the property from waste.
- Once the beneficiary takes lawful possession, he is entitled to the rents and profits from the property, even if the deed of trust does not contain a rents-and-profits clause.

The major disadvantage of taking possession of the property is that the beneficiary will be accountable to the trustor for any negligent injuries to the trustor's rights. (The beneficiary can avoid such liability by including a rents-and-profits clause in the deed of trust and requesting the appointment of a receiver to take possession of the property to collect rents and profits.)

Question: How should the beneficiary take possession of the property?

Answer: The beneficiary should simply get the trustor's consent to enter the property. A formal agreement between the parties is not necessary. Without consent, the beneficiary's entry onto the property without a court order could subject him to liability for trespassing and might also deprive him of any right to the rents and profits from the property.

Deeds In Lieu Of Foreclosure

Question: What is a deed in lieu of foreclosure?

Answer: A deed in lieu of foreclosure is a deed given by the trustor to the beneficiary to stop the foreclosure.

Question: What are the advantages and disadvantages to the beneficiary of taking a deed in lieu of foreclosure?

Answer: By accepting a deed in lieu of foreclosure, the beneficiary avoids the costs and delays of foreclosing. However, (a) junior creditors may argue that the deed in lieu of foreclosure is inadequate to wipe out their liens, (b) the trustor may later try to set the conveyance aside, and/or (c) the trustor's other creditors may argue that the conveyance was a "fraudulent conveyance" which jeopardizes their rights of successfully satisfying their claims against the trustor. For example, the California courts sometimes invalidate deed in lieu of foreclosure that are unfair to the trustor.

Question: What are the advantages and disadvantages to the trustor of giving a deed in lieu of foreclosure?

Answer: By giving a deed in lieu of foreclosure and thus stopping the foreclosure, the trustor avoids any further injury to his credit and insulates himself from any possible exposure to a deficiency judgment. However, the trustor will be denied any opportunity to retain the excess proceeds following a trustee's sale.

Question: Does a beneficiary who accepts a deed in lieu of foreclosure lose his right to wipe out junior liens through foreclosure?

Answer: Not necessarily. Even though the beneficiary probably takes the property subject to any junior liens created by the trustor, the beneficiary retains a right to bring a foreclosure action against those junior beneficiaries. However, it may be wiser for the beneficiary to ascertain that there are no junior liens prior to accepting the deed.

Question: Can a beneficiary take a deed in lieu of foreclosure at the time of making the loan?

Answer: No. A deed in foreclosure given at the time of making the loan or required to be given in the loan documents, effectively cuts off the trustor's redemption rights following default and is thus prohibited by law.

In Closing

"A successful man is one who can build a strong foundation with all the bricks thrown at him."

—*Unknown*

Summary

1. Farm area (foreclosure territory)
    - Default Service for you area.

2. Support Team
    - Title Company
    - Escrow Company
    - Mortgage Broker
    - Home Inspection Company
    - Termite Inspection

3. Prior to a Trustee Sale
    - Contact property owner by letter, CD or door knocking.
    - Fill out History Sheet
    - Have the owner get Beneficiary Statements from all Lenders (Demand for payoff)
    - Get written permission from the owner to talk to their Lenders
    - Get Property Profile from Title Company
    - Do three appraisals (do a drive by)

4. Lenders
    - Fill out your Math Formula Sheet
    - Call the Trustee Holder
    - Get Due on Sale Clause and Pre-payment Penalty waived
    - Call all Junior Lien Holders
    - Get discounted in writing with their demand sent to your Escrow Company to be paid off when sold (mention possible bankruptcy)

5. Open up Title Search
    - Get Home Inspections
    - Get Termite Report

6. Fill out Cost Break Down Sheet
    - Fill out Foreclosure Contract with owner (must be in homeowner's language if they don't read English, check you state for foreclosure contract)

7. Record Grant Deed
    - Bring first Trust Deed current
    - Rescission notice recorded

8. Fix and Sell

9. Cash out the homeowner after they have vacated the house.

10. If you are buying the house to live in or rent, keep payments current for several months and then refinance in your name. All discounted junior liens are paid off when you record the Grant Deed.

Having A Winning Attitude

To develop a winning attitude, you must become a dreamer again. What I mean by that is that most people have stopped dreaming. As a child, you were excited about life and about becoming somebody to be proud of. Once you get a taste of the real world, a lot of us have crawled into a shell and we began to develop an attitude that life is passing us by.

Become a dreamer again. To win in life you must be confident and excited about each and every day. I dreamed every day for years about how great it would feel to be financially independent. Those dreams kept me going when times were tough. I ultimately found out that being financially independent means being economically healthy and it's 100 times better than I ever dreamed it would be.

Developing a winning attitude may be the most important thing you will ever do for yourself in your lifetime because if you have a winning attitude, everything else you want can be accomplished.

You cannot buy a winning attitude; it is not for sale. You can't go to college and receive a degree in it. You aren't born with a winning attitude. You can either sabotage yourself or support yourself. You do have a choice. A winning attitude must be developed and maintained.

I trust I have helped you to begin dreaming again. I also trust I have shown you a vehicle and the motivation to become financially independent and economically healthy.

"You cannot travel within and stand still without"

Wealth and Success,

Cleo Katz

Cleo's Corner

*"Choose a job you love
and you will never have to
work a day in your life."*

—Cleo Katz

*Cleo standing on the staircase of the first REO Property she purchased
in 1984. She and her family lived in this house for twelve years!*

Cleo,

Thank you for allowing us to be part of your seminar. It's great to work with someone of the utmost integrity.

I'm looking forward to working with you in the future.

-Meagan Cole

Used with permisission of Meagan Cole.

NATIONAL COMMONWEALTH INSTITUTE
1500 ADAMS AVE. SUITE 105-152
COSTA MESA, CA 92626
(714) 557-3118

September 7, 1995

Cleo Katz
22383 Cass Ave.
Woodland Hills, CA 91364-3042

Dear Cleo:

Just a short note to say, "Thank You", for your outstanding presentation at our Commonwealth meeting on September 6, 1995. Your presentation was greatly enjoyed and very informative for all.

After your talk many people commented regarding the possibility of buying REO property. I am sure you will hear from some of our people

 Please feel free to attend our monthly meetings as our guest at any time. They are always on the first Wednesday of each month (except holidays). They start at 7pm at the Holiday Inn, 1850 S. Harbor Blvd. in Anaheim.

Look forward to seeing you in the near future. Thank you again for your fine talk.

Sincerely,

Jack H. Fullerton

Home foreclosures reach record numbers

BY MARTIN CRUTSINGER
Associated Press

WASHINGTON — A record number of homeowners got an unpleasant notice in their mailboxes this spring that their mortgages were being foreclosed.

The grim prospect is that thousands more of those notices will crop up in mailboxes in coming months as the steepest slump in housing in 16 years contributes to a widening mortgage crisis.

More than 2 million families are facing the prospect of seeing their adjustable mortgage payments rise sharply over the next two years, possibly to levels that many will be unable to pay.

The largest number of foreclosures and delinquencies have occurred in subprime mortgages, loans extended to people with weak credit histories. But quarterly data released Thursday by the Mortgage Bankers Association indicated the problem is now spreading to other types of mortgages.

The MBA report showed the number of homeowners who got foreclosure notices in the April-June quarter hit an all-time high of 0.65 percent, up from 0.58 percent in the first three months of the year. It marked the third consecutive quarter that a new record has been set.

The rising defaults in subprime mortgages have roiled global financial markets in recent weeks, send-

Reed Saxon/Associated Press

A home is advertised for sale at a foreclosure auction last month in Pasadena. The number of homeowners receiving foreclosure notices hit a record high in the spring, driven up by problems with subprime mortgages.

ing stock prices on a roller-coaster ride as investors wonder which big bank or hedge fund will be the next to report huge losses from subprime mortgages that were bundled into securities and resold to investors.

All About Foreclosures Opportunities

Foreclosure: a word which spells disaster to some and opportunity to others. Here are some answers to common questions.

**FORECLOSURE
SECRETS**

Cleo Katz

Question: What is a notice of default?

Answer: A notice of default is a recorded notice, prescribed by the California Civil Code, which begins the foreclosure process, gives public notice of the foreclosure, and triggers specific rights in favor of the trustor regarding his/her right to cure the default. The contents, format, and type size and style required of a notice of default are strictly prescribed by statute. Failure to comply may give the trustor grounds to challenge the trustee's sale. The description of the trustor's default must be identified with sufficient certainty. California law do not limit the trustee to foreclosing only on the known defaults identified in the notice of default; the notice of default may identify any other defaults which may occur prior to the sale date.

Question: Can anyone interested in the foreclosure of the property receive a notice of default?

Answer: Yes. At any time after a deed of trust is recorded, and prior to the recordation of a notice of default, any person wishing to receive a notice of default can acquire this right by recording a request for notice of default. A request for notice of default must be acknowledged, signed by the person making the request, and must substantially comply with a particular statutory format. This procedure is strongly recommended for persons who, thought they would be affected by a foreclosure, are nonetheless not otherwise entitled to a notice of default under California law (e.g., former owners of the property and guarantors of the debt). Within 10 days of recordation, a copy of the notice of default must either, (a) be published in a newspaper of general circulation in the county in which the property is located, or (b) be personally served on the trustor within those 10 days or before publication is completed. This requirement is applicable only if, (a) the deed of trust does not contain a request for notice of default by the trustor, or (b) the deed of trust does contain a trustor's request for notice of default, but does not contain an address and the trustor did not subsequently record a separate request for notice.

Question: When must a notice of default be given to the Office of the Controller?

Answer: If the state of California has a lien on the property for postponed property taxes under the Senior Citizens and Disabled Citizens Property Tax Postponement Law of 1977, the Office of the Controller must be given a copy of the notice of default and notice of sale if the foreclosing beneficiary's lien has priority over the state's tax lien.

Question: What is the effect of failing to provide a notice of default when required?

Answer: Failure to provide a required notice of default may not affect the validity of the sale if the affected person receives actual notice of the foreclosure. However, the trustee and beneficiary should assume that failure to provide a required notice, especially to the trustor, may void the sale.

Question: Can a beneficiary foreclose a deed of trust given by a trustor in active military service?

Answer: Generally, no. The Soldiers' and Sailors' Civil Relief Act of 1940 precludes most foreclosures of deeds of trust given by military personnel prior to entering into active duty, but only when their active duty responsibilities materially affect their ability to perform secured obligations.

Advantages of Purchasing Foreclosure Properties

**FORECLOSURE
SECRETS**

Cleo Katz

Buying from distressed owners is one of the best ways to obtain a property with built-in equity. In addition, you are saving the distressed person's credit and sharing the profit with them.

The seller can remain in the house and arrange for an orderly move during the time it is up for sale. Don't forget to ask for discounts from junior lien holders. They stand to be wiped out at a trustee's sale unless they can bring the senior liens current. Often the junior lien holder is willing to sell for a small percent of the face value of their lien.

You can also negotiate with lender before the trustee's sale. Some lenders are willing to give you good terms in exchange for taking over the loan in default. Lenders may be willing to help you take over a property since they are in the lending business, not the real estate business. When talking to a property owner, always ask them if they have a second trust deed, pool lien, patio lien, carpet lien, judgments or anything that they're paying on besides the first trust deed.

Tell them that you can't pay them until you have a title report on their property.

You may want to tell them, "I still might be able to buy your property so give me their names and I'll call them and see if I can make a deal with them, this way they won't lie to you and incur any unnecessary title charges."

All of their liens can be discounted for pennies on the dollar especially since most of these people are not in the real estate business.

Here is why liens can be discounted. One example: If a lienholder of a second trust deed or any kind of lien or judgment does nothing when the holder of a first trust deed forecloses on a property, this is what happens. The property goes to a trustee's sale on the 111th day of foreclosure. If no one bids on the property because there isn't enough equity, if it has an FHA or VA loan the government pays off the loan company in full for the amount of the first trust deed and wipes out anything behind it, such as a second trust deed or any liens. If someone bids at the trustee's sale, they have to pay off the first trust deed in cash and that wipes out everything behind it. If the holder of these junior liens does nothing to protect their investment, they get the same as the homeowner. *Nothing!*

You should structure every deal by satisfying the sellers needs first. By being fair, you leave a favorable impression which will generate other deals from referrals. Devote 100 percent of your effort to listening to the seller. You must be able to define the problem before negotiation can begin. Keep asking questions until his problem makes sense to you. Then proceed to find a solution.

Most good deals solve the sellers basic problem and allow the buyer to come away from the table with a profit. Most distressed properties need some cosmetic touch up.

Most properties in distress fail to sell when listed due to their poor "curb appeal." The seller has no money to make the necessary fix-up. With a little imagination, cash and work, you can bring the property up to "like new" condition and reap the rewards. You can also keep the property for rental purposes and receive long-term cash flow and tax benefits.

A Short Pay Off

FORECLOSURE
SECRETS

Cleo Katz

Some home owners are "up side down" ... Their existing loan balance(s) and other liens exceed the price they can get for their property.

Therefore, the only way they can sell, without going through foreclosure or bankruptcy, is to add cash to the escrow or get their lender(s) to agree to a short pay off. A short pay off is where the lender agrees to accept less than the outstanding balance as payment for the debt.

The lender will require a good reason to sell now, instead of waiting until the market recovers.

A lender may consider a short pay off if the reason for the sale is due to:

1. Unemployment
2. Divorce
3. Too many debts
4. Illness
5. Death
6. Relocation

A short sale allows the owners to sell their property at current market prices, turn the proceeds over to the lender, and perhaps survive with their credit intact or moderately damaged.

A short sale is strictly between the old owner and their lender. The new buyer can go to any lender. Title will show no trace of the former owner's financial problem.

Sellers who win a short sale agreement from their lenders should consult a tax adviser. A short sale may drive up a seller's tax liability.

What if the seller files bankruptcy or is already in bankruptcy?

Once the court determines that the property is over encumbered and there is no equity to pay other creditors, the property will eventually be removed from bankruptcy protection, and the lender will continue with the foreclosure. The "cram down" technique has been rejected by the courts for owner occupied 1-4 units, but not for commercial, indus-

trial, and apartments. Refer the seller to an attorney if the issue of bankruptcy arises.

Short pay off agreement

You need to make your offer contingent upon getting an agreement for a short pay off from the lender(s). The following should be in the purchase contract:

1. The offer is contingent upon the seller's ability to obtain a short pay off agreement from the lender.

2. Due to the need to obtain a short pay off agreement from the lender, the closing could take longer than normal.

3. A notice of default should be noted in the deposit receipt if filed by the lender.

A signed offer is when you approach the lender about a short pay off:

1. The request must come the seller in the form of a hardship letter.

2. Submit a copy of the buyer's offer, with the seller's acceptance contingent upon the lender's approval. Attach documents showing the buyer's ability to purchase.

3. Submit a rough estimate of the amount of short pay off it will take to close escrow.

4. Attach photos and comp sales.

Ask the lender(s) if they have a specific checklist when bringing in the offer.

Your offer to the lender(s) should be mailed by Federal Express and followed up with a phone call.

During the escrow period, keep in touch with the lender.

Paying the Original Mortgage or the Refinanced Mortgage

FORECLOSURE SECRETS

Cleo Katz

When funds are borrowed to buy a home, it is considered a "purchased-money" loan. That makes it a non-recourse loan under California law. If a borrower owes $ 300,000 on a home that's now worth only $200,000, the most that lender can do is take over the home. The lender cannot sue to get the difference from the borrower.

Many homeowners have refinanced due to the drop in mortgage rates in the past year. Most refis are recourse loans, the lender has the right to seek a deficiency judgment in court against a borrower if the foreclosed property is worth less than the debt still owed by the borrower. The lender could judicially foreclose on a house and seek an additional deficiency judgment from the homeowner. However, this method has rarely been employed by lenders because it can take more than a year.

The more common way is what's known as a non-judicial foreclosure, a lender directs a trustee to foreclose according to the lender's rights under the loan note and the deed of trust.

The internal revenue service treats the foreclosure like a sale of property for the debt. There is tax to be paid if the tax basis of the property is lower than the sale price. A homeowner could owe the IRS money even if their home is worth less than the property's mortgage.

When a loan is a recourse debt (a refinanced loan), the IRS will seek it's share of any cancellation of indebtedness. This tax can be avoided, if the debtor is insolvent or in bankruptcy. The lender will probably threaten a judicial foreclosure so that they can get a deficiency judgment. Most lenders will not follow through on such a threat, because of the time involved. A judicial foreclosure takes much longer than a non-judicial foreclosure, the borrower also gets a right of redemption.

That means that the borrower has a year to return to the lender with the money to buy back the home. This makes the home unsalable for a full year because the title is clouded.

On the non-judicial foreclosure there is a trustee sale on the 111th day conducted by the trustee. If the sale brings in more than the amount owed on the note, this money is transferred from the trustee to the trustor (borrower). If there's a deficiency, California law prohibits the lender in a non-judicial foreclosure from going after the borrower for the balance.

Learn About Deeds in Lieu of Foreclosures

FORECLOSURE SECRETS

Cleo Katz

What is a deed in lieu of foreclosure?

Answer: A deed in lieu of foreclosure is a deed given by the trustor to the beneficiary to stop the foreclosure.

What are the advantages and disadvantages to the beneficiary of taking a deed in lieu of foreclosure?

Answer: By accepting a deed in lieu of foreclosure, the beneficiary avoids the costs and delays of foreclosing. However, (a) junior creditors may argue that the deed in lieu of foreclosure is inadequate to wipe out their liens, (b) the trustor may later try to set the conveyance aside, and/or (c) the trustor's other creditors may argue that the conveyance was a "fraudulent conveyance" which jeopardizes their rights of successfully satisfying their claims against the trustor. In addition, the California courts sometimes invalidate deeds in lieu of foreclosure that are unfair to the trustor.

What are the advantages and disadvantages to the trustor of giving a deed in lieu of foreclosure?

Answer: By giving a deed in lieu of foreclosure and thus stopping the foreclosure, the trustor avoids any further injury to his/her credit and insulates himself/herself from any possible exposure to a deficiency judgment. However, the trustor will be denied any opportunity to retain the excess proceeds following a trustee's sale.

Does a beneficiary who accepts a deed in lieu of foreclosure lose his/her right to wipe out junior liens through foreclosure?

Answer: Not necessarily. Even though the beneficiary probably takes the property subject to any junior liens created by the trustor, the beneficiary retains a right to bring a foreclose action against those junior beneficiaries. However, it may be wiser for the beneficiary to ascertain that there are no junior liens prior to accepting the deed.

Can beneficiary take a deed in lieu of foreclosure at the time of making the loan?

Answer: No. A deed in lieu of foreclosure given at the time of making the loan or required to be given in the loan documents effectively cuts off the trustor's redemption rights following default and is thus prohibited by law.

What are the most common post-sale challenges to a trustee's sale?

Answer: The most common post-sale challenges to the sale include, (a) an action to set the sale aside, and (b) an action for damages against the beneficiary and/or trustee.

Under what circumstances may the trustee's sale be set aside or the beneficiary sued for damages?

Answer: The grounds for setting the sale aside or suing the beneficiary for damages are generally the same as for enjoining the sale. In addition, these actions may be based on irregularities in the sale.

Preliminary Title Made Simple

FORECLOSURE SECRETS

Cleo Katz

The principal use of the preliminary Report is to facilitate the issuance of a Title Insurance Policy. A "Prelimb: sets forth description of the property, owner of record, taxes, bonds, assessments, conditions, encumbrances, and exceptions which must be cured or included as exceptions such as a Bankruptcy field. By having as one of the conditions to purchasing a property a review of the Preliminary title Report, the buyer or lender may retreat from their commitment or insist the defects be corrected. Examples could be divorces, income tax liens, or persons who have similar names to those of either seller or buyer.

Heres where a name such as John Smith can be a problem, A final policy is issued and supersedes the Preliminary Report and creates a binding contract with the title company that all information is correct. The depth and detail of the title companies commitment depends upon which type of coverage is obtained. In California we have 2 different types of coverage. CLTA is standard coverage (California land Title Association).

This capacity that are off-record such as forgeries, incompetency of principals to the transaction, and alienage (limitations upon rights of certain people not living in the Unit-ed States). The CTLA does not cover mining claims, water and mineral rights, easements not shown by public record, zoning and governmental regulations on occupancy and use (American Land Title Association). Costs of title Insurance is based upon the amount of coverage (usually purchase price of the property). In California the seller pays for the title policy CLTA and the buyer for the ALTA. Title companies or your Realtor will provide you with a free chart to show costs. If you are buying property at a Trustee Sale or investing in a second or third Trust Deed then you will not be getting title insurance and only need the search done on what has been recorded on the property. In these two instances a Fleet Policy is what is needed from a title company.

California Civil Title Code

The intent of Civil Code 1695 is to ensure that the seller is informed of his rights, to ensure that all agreements are expressed in writing, to encourage fair dealings, to restrict unfair contract terms, to prohibit misleading representations, and to afford the homeowner an opportunity to rescind any agreement.

In order to be protected under the provisions of Civil Code 1695:

1. The property must be owner-occupied. (1 to 4 units)

2. A Notice of Default must be recorded against the property.

3. The buyer does not intend to occupy the premises as his principal place of residence

The most important requirement of Civil Code 1695 is the requirement that the homeowner must be given a five working day cooling off period after signing an agreement to sell his property.

This means that even after signing an agreement, the homeowner has five working days to cancel the agreement without penalty. The law is very specific regarding the format of the notification to the homeowner.

Failure to include the cancellation agreement required by Civil Code 1695, makes the contract voidable. The seller has two years in which to come back and declare the sale void and to reclaim his property.

Penalty

A violation of Civil Code 1695 could cost you up to a year in jail and a $ 10,000 fine, if, during the five working day cancellation period available to the seller, you:

1. Accept any instrument of conveyance from the seller.

2. Record any document concerning the property.

3. Transfer rights or encumber to a third party.

FORECLOSURE SECRETS

Cleo Katz

4. Make any untrue or misleading statements regarding:

a. The value of the property

b. The proceeds from the foreclosure sale.

c. The sale of the property to any other buyer.

Unconscionable Advantage

Section 1695.13 states that; "It is unlawful for any person to initiate, enter into, negotiate, or consummate any transaction involving residential real property in foreclosure, if such person, by the terms of the transaction, takes 'unconscionable advantage' of the property owner in foreclosure."

1. Avoid being classified as a Mortgage Foreclosure Consultant.

2. Act at all times as an equity purchaser.

3. Include and honor the five day cancellation period in your offer to purchase.

4. Express all agreements in writing.

5. Avoid misleading representations.

6. Admit and inform the seller (in writing and signed by him) that your offer to purchase should only be accepted as a last resort.

Note

The provisions of Civil Code 2945 and 1695 do not pertain to investor owned property in foreclosure, nor to an owner-occupant purchaser, nor do they pertain if the property is purchased at the foreclosure sale, or from the beneficiary following the foreclosure sale.

MARQUIS Who'sWho®   Who'sWho in America®

121 Chanlon Road • P.O. Box 2 • New Providence, N.J. 07974 U.S.A. • Phone: 1-800-621-9669 • Fax: 1-908-673-1179 • www.marquiswhoswho.com • E-Mail: america@renp.com

Founded by A. N. Marquis in 1899.
Publishers of the *original*
Who's Who in America®

Board of Advisors
*The current edition was compiled with
the assistance of the following
distinguished individuals.*

Mindy Aloff
Freelance Writer

William C. Anderson
Executive Director
American Academy of Environmental
Engineers

Steven C. Beering
President Emeritus
Purdue University

Willard L. Boyd
President Emeritus
Field Museum of Natural History

Dr. Thomas C. Dolan
President and CEO
American College of Healthcare
Executives

Charles C. Eldredge
Hall Distinguished Professor
of American Art
University of Kansas

Barbara Haskell
Curator
Whitney Museum of American Art

Thomas R. Horton
Former Chairman
American Management Association

Jill Krementz

Cleo Katz
Cleo Katz Seminars
22704 Ventura Blvd # 501
Woodland Hills, CA 91364

October 2002

Dear Cleo Katz:

Congratulations! Because of the reference value of your outstanding achievements, the editors of **Marquis Who's Who** have selected your biographical profile for inclusion in the forthcoming 57th Edition of **Who's Who in America**®. This unique compilation will chronicle the country's most accomplished men and women who are leading us forward in the 21st century.

In order to ensure the utmost
the enclosed galley p
Since this is th
rapidly

iFAQs

*Information and
Frequently Asked Questions*

State Foreclosure Information

State	Security Instrument	Foreclosure Type	Initial Setup	# of Months	Owner's Redemption Rights	Deficiency Judgment
Alabama	Mortgage	Non-judicial	Publication	1	12 Months	Allowed
Alaska	Trust Deed	Non-judicial	Notice of Default	3	None	Allowed
Arizona	Trust Deed	Non-judicial	Notice of Sale	3	None	Allowed
Arkansas	Mortgage	Judicial	Complaint	4	None	Allowed
California	Trust Deed	Non-judicial	Notice of Default	4	None	Prohibited
Colorado	Trust Deed	Non-judicial	Notice of Default	2	75 Days	Allowed
Connecticut	Mortgage	Strict	Complaint	5	None	Allowed
Delaware	Mortgage	Judicial	Complaint	3	None	Allowed
District of Columbia	Trust Deed	Non-judicial	Notice of Default	2	None	Allowed
Florida	Mortgage	Judicial	Complaint	5	None	Allowed
Georgia	Security Deed	Non-judicial	Publication	2	None	Allowed
Hawaii	Mortgage	Non-judicial	Publication	3	None	Allowed
Idaho	Trust Deed	Non-judicial	Notice of Default	5	None	Allowed
Illinois	Mortgage	Judicial	Complaint	7	None	Allowed
Indiana	Mortgage	Judicial	Complaint	5	3 Months	Allowed
Iowa	Mortgage	Judicial	Petition	5	6 Months	Allowed
Kansas	Mortgage	Judicial	Complaint	4	6-12 Months	Allowed
Kentucky	Mortgage	Judicial	Complaint	6	None	Allowed
Louisiana	Mortgage	Judicial	Petition	2	None	Allowed
Maine	Mortgage	Judicial	Complaint	6	None	Allowed
Maryland	Trust Deed	Non-judicial	Notice	2	None	Allowed
Massachusetts	Mortgage	Judicial	Complaint	3	None	Allowed
Michigan	Mortgage	Non-judicial	Publication	2	6 Months	Allowed
Minnesota	Mortgage	Non-judicial	Publication	2	6 Months	Prohibited
Mississippi	Trust Deed	Non-judicial	Publication	2	None	Prohibited
Missouri	Trust Deed	Non-judicial	Publication	2	None	Allowed
Montana	Trust Deed	Non-judicial	Notice	5	None	Prohibited
Nebraska	Mortgage	Judicial	Petition	5	None	Allowed
Nevada	Trust Deed	Non-judicial	Notice of Default	4	None	Allowed
New Hampshire	Mortgage	Non-judicial	Notice of Sale	2	None	Allowed
New Jersey	Mortgage	Judicial	Complaint	3	10 Days	Allowed
New Mexico	Mortgage	Judicial	Complaint	4	None	Allowed
New York	Mortgage	Judicial	Complaint	4	None	Allowed
North Carolina	Trust Deed	Non-judicial	Notice Hearing	2	None	Allowed
North Dakota	Mortgage	Judicial	Complaint	3	60 Days	Prohibited
Ohio	Mortgage	Judicial	Complaint	5	None	Allowed
Oklahoma	Mortgage	Judicial	Complaint	4	None	Allowed
Oregon	Trust Deed	Non-judicial	Notice of Default	5	None	Allowed
Pennsylvania	Mortgage	Judicial	Complaint	3	None	Allowed
Rhode Island	Mortgage	Non-judicial	Publication	2	None	Allowed
South Carolina	Mortgage	Judicial	Complaint	6	None	Allowed
South Dakota	Mortgage	Judicial	Complaint	3	180 Days	Allowed
Tennessee	Trust Deed	Non-judicial	Publication	2	None	Allowed
Texas	Trust Deed	Non-judicial	Publication	2	None	Allowed
Utah	Trust Deed	Non-judicial	Notice of Default	4	None	Allowed
Vermont	Mortgage	Judicial	Complaint	7	None	Allowed
Virginia	Trust Deed	Non-judicial	Publication	2	None	Allowed
Washington	Trust Deed	Non-judicial	Notice of Default	4	None	Allowed
West Virginia	Trust Deed	Non-judicial	Publication	2	None	Prohibited
Wisconsin	Mortgage	Judicial	Complaint	Varies	None	Allowed
Wyoming	Mortgage	Non-judicial	Publication	2	3 Months	Allowed

Check with your local law library for the most up-to-date information regarding foreclosure procedures in your area.

LIFE OF AN ESCROW

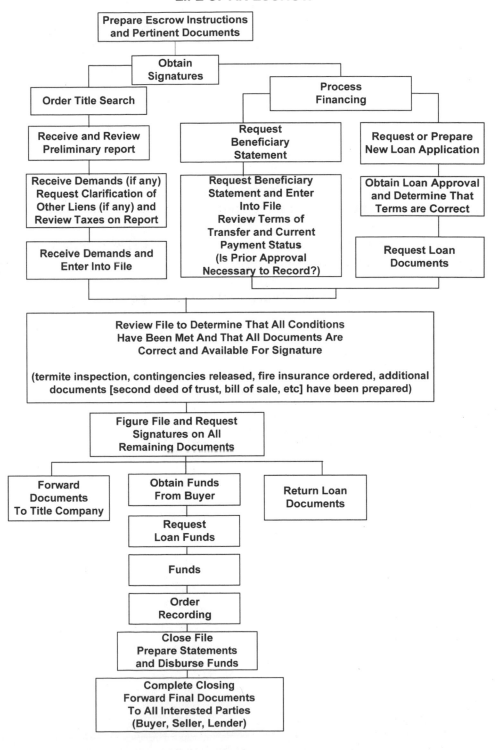

GUIDELINES TO OPENING AN ESCROW

To open escrow, deliver to your escrow holder the following information:

1. Buyer's name and vesting (How Buyer will take title to subject property).

2. Buyer's present address, home phone number and office number and/ or message number.

3. Seller's name.

4. Seller's present address, if not property address, and home phone number and office number and/or message number.

5. Address of property- house number, and if the same is Avenue, Street, Lane, etc., City, and Zip Code.

6. As much of legal description and parcel number as possible.

7. Financing

    a. New Loan

        1. Amount

        2. Name, address, phone number and name of loan agent

        3. Interest Rate

        4. Loan Fee

    b. Secondary Financing

        1. Amount

        2. Interest Rate

        3. Due Date

        4. Late Charges

        5. Acceleration Clause

6. Request for notice of default

7. Name, address, phone number and name of loan agent if not purchased money

c. Assumption of Existing Loan

1. Amount of approximate unpaid balance

2. Name address, and loan number of existing Lender

3. Interest rate- will it remain the same or be adjusted?

4. Loan assumption fees and/or charges assessed by existing Lender

d. Land Contract or All–Inclusive

1. Name(s) of underlying Beneficiary(s) an approximate unpaid balance(s)

2. Principal amount of Land Contract or All-Inclusive Note/Trust Deed

3. Interest Rate

4. Due Date

5. Late Charges

6. Request for Notice of Default

7. Acceleration Clause

8. Special terms or conditions

ADVISE THAT PARTIES SEEK LEGAL ADVICE

8. Name(s) address(s), and loan number(s) of any loan(s) or encumbrance(s) to be paid off at the close of escrow.

9. Specific contingency(s), or conditions which escrow is subject to and the date said contingency(s) shall expire and be deemed approved.

10. City Ordinance: In Los Angeles #144,942 and #3153,637 (smoke detectors), check in to the Department of Building and Safety and signature on a 9a Application of party responsible for installation of smoke detectors.

11. Termite Inspection Report, if applicable.

12. Additional instruction pursuant to sale not mentioned above.

13. Memo Items Agreed Upon Between Buyer And Seller Outside Of Escrow's Jurisdiction:

    a. Personal property; e.g., window treatment, fireplace, equipment etc.

    b. Warranties

    c. Date of possession to Buyer

14. Fire Insurance - Assume existing or new policy.

    a. Name of agent and insurance company, phone number, policy number (if assumed) and verification to escrow holder if property located in a brush area that may require California Fair Plan to write policy.

15. Condominiums Only - Provide name and address of Homeowners Association and amount of monthly dues.

16. Name of Title Company and representative to credit order.

17. Preliminary Chance of Ownership Form - make sure it is filled in completely and signed by County Recorder.

Frequently Asked Questions

The following are answers to some of the most commonly posed questions regarding purchases of foreclosures.

Question: Are there closing costs when buying a foreclosure?

Answer: Yes: the cost of the title insurance policy and the cost of recording your deed.

Question: Will I need a lawyer when buying a foreclosure?

Answer: The terms are set; the lawyer will not be able to change them. Your title insurance policy is the best protection.

Question: Once you put your bid in at the foreclosure sale, can the homeowner still get the property back before you put down the balance?

Answer: No. Once the sale goes forth, it is final.

Question: I'm concerned about the permanence of the foreclosure sale I'm contemplating. Doesn't the former owner have the right to buy the house back within a year?

Answer: That's what's known as a "right of redemption." Such rights do not exist in foreclosure sales, although they do in tax sales of sheriff's sales.

Question: How do you get people out of the property if they continue to occupy after the sale? Won't the bank take care of that?

Answer: The bank will not handle this for you. This situation is similar to a tenant holdover conflict in which a landlord wishes to eject a tenant from a rental property. Offer move out cash, "cash for keys."

Question: Can I get a GI mortgage on a foreclosure?

Answer: Not on a foreclosed property bought at public auction. Such sales are "all cash," although you might be able to get a GI mortgage on a bank-owned foreclosure.

Question: Why shouldn't banks look forward to selling out properties with small mortgages so they can make money on the sale?

Answer: Real Estate Owned is an item banks would rather not have on their financial statements. They'd much prefer to have these properties sold to third parties. Banks can not collect only the sums legally due them. They do not share in any coverage that may arise from the property at the Trustee Sale.

Question: I've gone to a house that was in the process of being foreclosed, but the occupant wouldn't let me in to see the place. How can I get a look before placing a bid?

Answer: You may be limited to an exterior assessment. On the other hand, if the house is vacant, you can always try calling the bank. You'll probably get in for a look; after all, the bank wants to sell the property.

Question: Where can I learn about properties being foreclosed?

Answer: If there is no publication in your area that covers these matters, you can go to the county courthouse where the notices are posted.

Question: Where are foreclosure sales held?

Answer: The notice of publication will indicate where the sale will be held. Typically, sales are held on the steps of the courthouse. You must be prompt in arriving at foreclosure sales.

Question: Let's assume that I am the successful bidder at the sale. Am I obligated to pay up any other creditors of the party being foreclosed?

Answer: Only if the recording of their claims precedes the recording of the party who is doing the foreclosure.

Question: Suppose that a second mortgage is being foreclosed and that I win the bid. Do I have to pay up the first mortgage completely?

Answer: No, although if it is in arrears you will have to bring it current. You assume the responsibility for it when you buy the property at the foreclosure sale.

Question: Will the bank fix the neglect of the past owner?

Answer: The bank won't do anything to property it doesn't own except board it up to prevent vandalism. If you buy a previously foreclosed property from the banks. REOs, they are a different story. In such a case, the bank owns the property. You can ask for anything. The answer will depend on the individual circumstances surrounding the property.

Question: If a property is being foreclosed, could I arrange to buy it before the sale from the owner and continue his mortgage?

Answer: If you could get an arrangement for a deed from the homeowner, you could talk to the bank about reinstating the mortgage and assuming it.

Question: I'd like to simplify things. Is there a rule of thumb to help me determine what percentage of value I should pay for a foreclosure?

Answer: No. Too many variables—condition, salability, location, financing, and taxes, to name only a few, come into play.

Question: If the foreclosed property has improvements that were never finally inspected and there are no certificates of occupancy for them, will the bank furnish these certificates at the sale?

Answer: No. This is one of the perils of buying a foreclosure. In order to get a permanent mortgage loan on the property, you will have to get certificates. This is usually not a major setback, but you will have to do some legwork and handle some minor expenses associated with the process.

Question: What are the rights of tenants under a lease?

Answer: If the lease precedes the date of the mortgage being foreclosed, the tenant stays. Leases made after this date are invalidated by the foreclosure process. Consult your attorney for more details; remember that local laws will vary when it comes to extricating tenants from property to which you have a legal right.

Question: I've heard that the real estate brokers have an inside track on the good foreclosures. Is this true?

Answer: Foreclosure sales are conducted by a referee who is assigned by the court. The bank has no say in the selection of this person.

Question: If the prior owner didn't pay the taxes on a foreclosed property, does the successful bidder have to pay them?

Answer: No. If the taxes weren't paid, the county could sell the property out from under the bank's mortgage lien. Banks pay the amounts due to municipalities and sell the property with all tax payments current.

Question: How does a tax sale differ from a foreclosure sale?

Answer: When the public authorities offer a property for sale to satisfy a tax lien, the successful bidder buys the right to own the property if the property owner does not repay him. This is not the case at a foreclosure sale.

Question: If Seller is a widow or widower - has or will property be probated?

Answer: If not subject to probate, escrow holder will probably need Affidavit of Death of Joint Tenant and/or Inheritance Tax Lien Release.

If Seller is in title as a married man, a married woman or no status spouse may need to execute a Quitclaim Deed, or participate in transaction as a seller.

If Buyer is to acquire title as a married man, as his sole and separate property, or a married woman, as her sole and separate property, spouse will have to execute a Quitclaim Deed.

If Seller holds title as Trustee for a living Trust, or if Buyer is to acquire title as Trustee for Living Trust: Title Company and/or Lender may require copies of Trust, and statement from Trustee that Trust is still in effect and has not been amended.

If a parent and a child (over 18) are to acquire title in any combination, that relationship will be stated in addition to marital status.

If the Seller is reselling property within one year, did the acquire it with a Binder. If so, title policy must be obtained through original issuing title company

If you do not know Buyer's vesting, no Grant Deed can be drawn.

In the event property is in a brush area, allow six (6) weeks for fire insurance policy. Advise escrow early in the transaction.

Any inquires to escrow holder must be made by a Principal to the transaction of their Real Estates Agents. Buyer's or Seller's attorneys, accountants, ex-wife are not entitled to information without clear direction from principal.

FORECLOSURE PROCESS THROUGH REO SALE

I. INTIAL STEPS

Lender or attorney initiates
foreclosure by transmitting relevant
documents to T.D.

If you are servicing the loan
and not the beneficiary, the
Notice of Default,
Substitution of Trustee and
other documents are prepared and
sent on for the beneficiary's
signature

If you are the beneficiary,
having to sed the documents to
you can be eliminated by signing
a Limited Power of Attorney
or Agency Agreement which gives
T.D. the authorization to sign the
documents and start a foreclosure

Return signed documents to T.D.

**II. PRE-PUBLICATION
PERIOD**

Notice of Default, in most cases,
is recorded within 24-48 hours

Trustee's Sale Guarantee is ordered
from title company

10-day Notices are mailed

Trustee's Sale Guarantee is reviewed and
the required on-month notices are mailed

If loan has not been paid off or
reinstated within 3 months from when
the Notice of Default was recorded,
the lender can authorize publication of
the Notice of Trustee's Sale
(after publication)

III. REINSTATEMENT

Borrower may cure the default
at any time after the Notice
of Default was recored up to
5 business days prior to the
day of sale

If the sale is postponed for
more than 5 business days, the
right of rein statement is
revived and will continue up to
5 busiiness days before the
next schedule sale date

IV. PUBLICATION PERIOD

T.D will prepare, record and coordinate the required postings and publishing of the Notice of Trustee's Sale

The Trustee's Sale is scheduled for approximately 25-30 days after the pre-publication period has expired

Record Notice of Trustee's Sale is mailed to all entitled parties

V. TRUSTEE'S SALE

T.D. conducts a Public Trustee's Sale

Property sold to outsider bidder

Property to revert back to beneficiary

VI. AFTER THE TRUSTEE'S SALE

Trustee's Deed Upon Sale is prepared and recorded and sent to the County Recorder for recording

The Recorder mails the recorded Trustee's Deed back to the successful bidder or to the beneficiary if there were no bidders at the sale

TD informs T.D. REO of property to be auctioned

T.D. REO contacts lender or attorney to discuss non-producing asset which is scheduled for auction

T.D. REO informed of outcome of Trustee's Sale

T.D. REO is assigned management of property by lender or attorney

T.D REO obtains property inspection report

T.D. REO coordinates eviction, if necessary

T.D. REO makes utilities operational: contracts for gardening, pool, spa repair, maintenance

T.D. REO installs/replaces locks; supervising contracted vendors

T.D. REO orders property appraisal(s) if required

T.D. REO prepares Broker Price Opinion Package within 7 days including:
-photographs
-property value estimates
-termite, roof and pool reports
-recommendations of needed repairs
-enhancement recommendations
-recommendations on financing terms

Marketing plan prepared for property

T.D. REO places listing with licensed real estate broker who meets T.D. REO's written standards

T.D. REO manages real estate broker(s), vendors, escrow companies until close of escrow

Property inspections performed monthly

Bi-monthly written status reports are provided to the lender

T.D. REO screens and forwards all offers and recommendations on a timely basis

T.D. REO manages property and transaction through close of escrow

END

$ $

Worksheets

PROPERTY HISTORY SHEET

CALL/VISIT DATES:

1. _____ 2. _____ 3. _____ 4. _____ 5. _____ 6. _____

NEIGHBORHOOD (determine distances from the following):

SCHOOLS: ELEMENTARY _____ HIGH _____ COLLEGE _____

SHOPPING _____ PARKS _____ FREEWAYS _____ FIRE STATION _____

AREA: POOL _____ MARINA _____ TENNIS _____ GOLF _____

CLUBHOUSE _____ SECURITY _____ TREES _____ GROOMING _____

BIKE/JOG TRAILS _____ STREET PARKING _____ SIDEWALKS _____

STREET LIGHTING _____ UNDERGROUND ULTILITIES _____

STORM DRAINS _____ SALE/RENT/LEASE SIGNS _____

EXTERNAL PROPERTY: GENERAL APPEARANCE _____ PAINT _____

LOT LOCATION _____ SIZE _____ # OF STORIES _____ STYLE _____

TYPE OF CONSTRUCTION ___ LANDSCAPING ___ SPRINKLER SYSTEM ___

FENCES _____ POOL/HEATER/FILTER _____ SPA _____

PATIO _____ DECK _____ GARAGE _____ ROOF _____ VIEW _____

SEWER _____ SEPTIC _____ OTHER _____

LAND LEASEHOLD _____

INTERNAL PROPERTY: LIVING AREA SQ.FT. _____ AGE _____

TOTAL ROOMS _____ BEDROOMS _____ BATHROOMS _____

OTHER ROOMS _____ BASEMENT _____

FIREPLACE _____ A/C _____ SMOKE DETECTORS _____

BUILT-INS _____ CONDITION OF GLASS _____

KITCHEN COMPACTOR _____ DISHWASHER _____ RANGE _____

OVEN _____ REFRIDGERATOR _____ DISPOSAL _____

OTHER _____

DEMAND FOR PAY-OFF SHEET
(Beneficiary Statement from Lender(s))

Default Date: _____

Foreclosure Date: _____

Trustee Sale Date: _____

GRANT DEED: _____ Dated: _____
(Homeowner's Name)

FIRST TRUST DEED: _____ Dated: _____
(Lender's Name)

Loan #: _____ Lender's Phone # _____

Last Date Paid: _____ Amount: $_____ Loan Type: _____

Monthly Payment: $_____

JUNIOR TRUST DEED (2ND): _____ Issue Date: _____
(Lender's Name)

Lien Type: _____

Loan #: _____ Lender's Phone # _____

Last Date Paid: _____ Amount: $_____ Monthly Payment: $_____

JUNIOR TRUST DEED (3RD): _____ Issue Date: _____

Lien Type: _____

Loan #: _____ Lender's Phone # _____

Last Date Paid: _____ Amount: $_____ Monthly Payment: $_____

JUNIOR TRUST DEED (4TH): _____ Issue Date: _____

Lien Type: _____

Loan #: _____ Lender's Phone # _____

Last Date Paid: _____ Amount: $_____ Monthly Payment: $_____

INSURANCE: _____ Issue Date: _____
(Insurance Company Name)

Policy #: _____ Agents Phone #: _____

Includes: Fire: _____ Flood _____ Earthquake _____ Other _____

EXTENSIONS:

VA/FHA Extension End Date: _____ Waived: _____
(Homeowners in foreclosure with VA/FHA loans can possibly get additional time)

COMPARATIVE MARKET ANALYSIS TABLE

PROPERTIES THAT HAVE SOLD	STYLE	AGE	TAXES	TOTAL SQ. FT.	BED ROOMS (No.)	BATHS (No.)	DINING ROOM (?)	DEN OR FAMILY ROOM(?)	HEAT/ COOL (TYPE)	LISTED PRICE	SOLD PRICE
1.											
2.											
3.											

Check your local newspapers for homes that are currently on the market, and see what the asking prices are. Compare your property to those listed using the Comparative Market Analysis Table. Comparative Market Analysis is always based on the "Sold Price".

COST BREAKDOWN SHEET

(Get from Beneficiary Statement, which you get from Homeowner's Lenders)

Homeowner's Name: _____   Telephone # _____

Property Address: _____

Date Default Filed: _____   End Date: _____

Trustee: _____   Telephone # _____

	Loan	Type	% Interest	Original Amount	Number of Payments	Annual Taxes	Balance as of Date	Delinquent Payments	Late Charges	Total
1										0
2										0
3										0
4										0
5										0
6										0
7										0
8										0
TOTALS	0	0	0	0	0	0	0	0	0	0

Lender/Lien

Total Delinquency $ _____   Property Sale Price $ _____
(what I plan to sell for)

Trustee's Fees $ _____   Minus Loan Balance $ _____

Loan Transfer Fee $ _____   Minus "Cure" Outlay $ _____
(Late Fees/Penalties/etc.)

Escrow/Title Co. Fees $ _____   Minus Selling Costs $ _____

Misc Charges $ _____
(add $2000+/more for higher priced homes)

Fix-Up Cost Estimate $ _____   Net Proceeds $ _____
(Licensed Contractor)

Total Buyer Outlay $ _____

Estimate of Market Value (Comps) $ _____

Address of Comps (From Title Co. Listing Sheets)   Cost per Sq. Ft.   Market Value

1 _____

2 _____

3 _____

Simple Formula For
Buying And Selling Property

You must know before you make an offer what you want to pay for the property. This formula may be used for large and small purchases.

You work backward from the price you want to sell the property for. You factor in the profit you would like to make plus all of your expenses.

1. A property profile is the best way to get the true market value of the property being considered. This short report can be obtained from a title company in the area. Ask for customer service, and a customer service representative will help you by sending you this free short report which should include properties recently sold in the area. Of course, you are expected to order your title insurance policy from them when this is eventually needed.

Comparative Market Analysis
(Compared with similar properties that have been sold in the area)
>   A. Style
>   B. Age
>   C. Taxes
>   D. Total Square Footage
>   E. No. of bedrooms
>   F. No. of baths
>   G. Dining room
>   H. Den or family room
>   I. Heat/cool (type/age)
>   J. Listed price
>   K. Actual sale price

2. Subtract the profit you want to make on the property. Allow 2 to 4 months to fix-up and sell.

3. Subtract the selling agent's commission. You may elect to sell the house yourself then you do not need to include a selling agent's commission.

4. Subtract the fix-up costs. Your contractor can give you an estimated break-down.

5. Deduct your carrying costs. This has to be estimated, since you don't know the exact selling date. Include monthly mortgage payments, taxes, utilities, and insurance.

6. If you bought the house from homeowners who were in foreclosure, subtract back-payments, trustee fees, and late charges. Subtract closing costs if you are buying a non-foreclosure (these vary from state to state).

7. Subtract the "cash-out" to the foreclosure homeowner (remember the six magic words to a home owner: "You Can Share In The Profits").

Math Formula
Worksheet

Building Equity Into A Property

Example of when a first trust deed or mortgage is foreclosing and there are Junior Lien(s) that can be discounted

Your Expected Selling Price $500,000.00

Subtract:

Desired Net Profit $35,000.00

Selling Commission (5%) $ 25,000.00
(optional)

Fix Up Costs $ 12,000.00

Foreclosure and/or Closing Costs $ 6,000.00

Loans $550,000.00
    1st Trust Deed/Mortgage $400,000.00
    2nd Jr. Lien Holder $150,000.00
    (Discount the second by $133,000.00 and give the 2nd Jr. Lien Holder $17,000.00.
    If there are additional Lien Holders, spread the discount over all Lien Holders)

Homeowner Cash-Out $ 5,000.00

Total Expenses (before discounting Jr. Liens) $630,000.00

Total Discount Offered (Total minus Your Expected Selling Price) $133,000.00

Top Offer to Make on This Property   **$417,000.00**
(After all of the above expenses are subtracted, this is your top offer to lien holders)
(The first $400,000.00 to the 1st Trust Deed/Mortgage Holder and the remaining
$17,000.00 goes the the 2nd Junior Lien Holder)

Math Formula Worksheet

Building Equity Into A Property

Example of when a first trust deed or mortgage is foreclosing and there are Junior Lien(s) that can be discounted

Your Expected Selling Price $_____

Subtract:

Desired Net Profit $_____

Selling Commission (5%) $_____
(optional)

Fix Up Costs $_____

Foreclosure and/or Closing Costs $_____

Loans $_____
    1st Trust Deed/Mortgage $_____
    2nd Jr. Lien Holder $_____
    3rd Jr. Lien Holder $_____ (if appropriate)
    (Discount the second and/or third by $_____ and give the
    2nd Jr. Lien Holder $_____ and 3rd Jr. Lien Holder $_____)
    (If there are additional Lien Holders, spread the discount over all Lien Holders)

Homeowner Cash-Out $_____

Total Expenses (before discounting Jr. Liens) $_____

Total Discount Offered (Total minus Your Expected Selling Price) $_____

Top Offer to Make on This Property $_____
(After all of the above expenses are subtracted, this is your top offer to lien holders)
(The first $_____ to the 1st Trust Deed/Mortgage Holder and the remaining
$_____ goes the the 2nd and/or 3rd Junior Lien Holders)

Sample
Real Estate
Agreement Forms

Used with permission from the California Board Of Realtors®
(Contact your local Board Of Realtors for the appropriate forms in your state)

HOME EQUITY EXPLANATION AND AGENCY AGREEMENT
(FOR USE WHEN AN INVESTOR BUYER USES THE ATTACHED AGREEMENT TO
OFFER TO PURCHASE AN OWNER-OCCUPIED RESIDENTIAL DWELLING
AGAINST WHICH A NOTICE OF DEFAULT HAS BEEN RECORDED)
(C.A.R. Forms HEAA AND NODPA 1/06)

CALIFORNIA
ASSOCIATION
OF REALTORS ®

If this contract has been negotiated primarily in a language other than English, this Agreement must be translated into that other language under California Civil Code §1695.2.

Date _____, at _____, California.

1. AGREEMENT SUBJECT TO CIVIL CODE:
The attached Purchase Agreement is to be used when an investor buyer offers to purchase a residential dwelling containing one to four units, one of which is owner-occupied, and a Notice of Default has been recorded against the Property. The purchase is subject to Civil Code §§1695 through 1695.17. If certain provisions of those code sections are violated: **(i)** Buyer may be responsible for actual and exemplary damages and attorney fees and costs incurred by Seller, a civil penalty of up to $2,500 and a fine of up to $25,000; **(ii)** Buyer may be subject to imprisonment for not more than one year; and **(iii)** the transaction may be rescinded by the Seller up to two years after Close Of Escrow.

2. SELLER CANCELLATION RIGHT:
Seller may cancel the attached Purchase Agreement until midnight on the fifth business day following the day on which Seller signs the attached Purchase Agreement or until 8:00 a.m. on the day scheduled for the sale of the Property pursuant to a power of sale conferred in a deed of trust, whichever occurs first.

3. BUYER RESTRICTIONS PRIOR TO EXPIRATION OF CANCELLATION RIGHT:
Until Seller's right to cancel the attached Purchase Agreement has lapsed, Buyer shall not: (i) accept from Seller an execution of, or induce Seller to execute, any instrument conveying any interest in the Property; (ii) record any instrument signed by Seller; (iii) transfer or encumber or purport to transfer or encumber any interest in the Property to any third party; or (iv) pay Seller any consideration.

4. REAL ESTATE AGENT LICENSE AND BONDING:
Civil Code §1695.17 requires an Equity Purchaser's Representative (Buyer's agent) to hold a valid real estate license and a bond equal to twice the fair market value of the Property. If the Equity Purchaser's Representative fails to comply with the above requirements, the contract is voidable by Seller and can subject the Equity Purchaser's Representative to damages. An Equity Purchaser's Representative is defined, in part, as a person who solicits, induces or causes the Property owner to transfer title. In order to reduce the risk of being considered an Equity Purchaser's Representative for any transaction resulting from the attached Purchase Agreement, a real estate agent who introduces a Buyer to the Property should terminate any agency relationship with Buyer prior to Buyer's presentation of the attached Purchase Agreement or any other activity by the agent designed to solicit, induce or cause the Property owner to transfer title.

5. AGENCY
   A. NO REPRESENTATION OF BUYER: Neither Listing agent nor Referral Licensee (as confirmed below) represents Buyer in the transaction specified in the attached Purchase Agreement. Buyer acknowledges receipt of a Buyer Non-Agency Agreement (C.A.R. Form BNA) from Listing Agent and a Termination of Buyer Agency Agreement (C.A.R. Form TBA) from Referral Licensee. Referral Licensee should stop representing Buyer and should avoid any communication with Seller and Seller's Agent on behalf of Buyer signing below.
   B. DISCLOSURE: Seller acknowledges prior receipt of C.A.R. Form AD "Disclosure Regarding Real Estate Agency Relationships."
   C. POTENTIALLY COMPETING SELLERS: Seller acknowledges receipt of a disclosure of the possibility of multiple representation by Broker. This disclosure may be part of a listing agreement or separate document (C.A.R. Form DA). Seller understands that Broker representing Seller may also represent other sellers with competing properties of interest to this Buyer.
   D. CONFIRMATION: The following agency relationships are hereby confirmed for the transaction specified in the attached Purchase Agreement:
   (1) Listing Agent _____ (Print Firm Name)
   is the agent of the Seller exclusively.
   (2) Other Agent (Referral Licensee)_____ (Print Firm Name)
   is a Referral Licensee Only. Buyer and Seller acknowledge and agree that Referral Licensee has merely introduced Buyer to the Property and does not represent Buyer or Seller in the transaction specified in the attached Purchase Agreement. Buyer further acknowledges and agrees that any agency relationship with Referral Licensee, whether existing under a written or oral agreement or by implication, is terminated for this Property no later than the date of Buyer's signature on this Home Equity Explanation and Agency Agreement. Neither Listing Agent nor Referral Licensee are parties to the Purchase Agreement between Buyer and Seller.

HEAA 1/06 (PAGE 1 OF 2) Print Date

Buyer's Initials (_____)(_____)
Seller's Initials (_____)(_____)

| Reviewed by _____ Date _____ |

HOME EQUITY EXPLANATION AND AGENCY AGREEMENT (HEAA PAGE 1 OF 2)

Property Address: _____ Date: _____

6. REFERRAL LICENSE COMPENSATION:
If Buyer signing below purchases the Property identified in the attached Purchase Agreement, Listing Broker agrees to pay Referral Licensee and Referral Licensee agrees to accept, out of Listing Broker's proceeds in escrow: (i) the amount specified in the MLS, provided Referral Licensee is a Participant of the MLS in which the Property is offered for sale or a reciprocal MLS; or (ii) ☐ (if checked) the amount specified in a separate written agreement (C.A.R. Form CBC) between Listing Broker and Referral Licensee:

Referral Licensee (Broker)_____ DRE Lic. # _____
By _____ DRE Lic. # _____ Date _____
Address _____ City _____ State _____ Zip_____
Telephone _____ Fax _____ E-mail _____

Real Estate Broker (Listing Firm) _____ DRE Lic. # _____
By _____ DRE Lic. # _____ Date _____
Address _____ City _____ State _____ Zip_____
Telephone _____ Fax _____ E-mail _____

Buyer _____ Date _____

(Print name)
Address _____ City _____ State _____ Zip_____
Telephone _____ Fax _____ E-mail _____

Buyer _____ Date _____

(Print name)
Address _____ City _____ State _____ Zip_____
Telephone _____ Fax _____ E-mail _____

Seller _____ Date _____

(Print name)
Address _____ City _____ State _____ Zip_____
Telephone _____ Fax _____ E-mail _____

Seller _____ Date _____

(Print name)
Address _____ City _____ State _____ Zip_____
Telephone _____ Fax _____ E-mail _____

Published and Distributed by:
REAL ESTATE BUSINESS SERVICES, INC.
a subsidiary of the California Association of REALTORS®
525 South Virgil Avenue, Los Angeles, California 90020

HEAA 1/06 (PAGE 2 OF 2)

Reviewed by _____ Date _____

EQUAL HOUSING
OPPORTUNITY

HOME EQUITY EXPLANATION AND AGENCY AGREEMENT (HEAA PAGE 2 OF 2)

NOTICE OF DEFAULT PURCHASE AGREEMENT
(FOR USE WHEN AN INVESTOR BUYER OFFERS TO PURCHASE
AN OWNER-OCCUPIED RESIDENTIAL DWELLING AGAINST WHICH
A NOTICE OF DEFAULT HAS BEEN RECORDED)
(C.A.R. Form NODPA, 1/06)

1. **OFFER:**
   A. **THIS IS AN OFFER FROM** _____ ("Buyer").
   B. **THE REAL PROPERTY TO BE ACQUIRED is** described as _____
      _____, Assessor's Parcel No. _____, situated
      in _____, County of _____, California, ("Property").
   C. **THE PURCHASE PRICE** offered is _____
      _____ Dollars $ _____.
   D. **CLOSE OF ESCROW** shall occur on _____ (date) (or ☐ _____ Days After Acceptance).
2. **FINANCE TERMS:** Obtaining the loans below is a contingency of this Agreement unless: (i) either 2K or 2L is
   checked below; or (ii) otherwise agreed in writing. Buyer shall act diligently and in good faith to obtain the
   designated loans. Obtaining deposit, down payment and closing costs is not a contingency. Buyer represents
   that funds will be good when deposited with Escrow Holder.
   A. **INITIAL DEPOSIT:** Buyer has given a deposit in the amount of . . . . $ _____
      to _____, by personal check
      (or ☐ _____), made payable to
      _____, which shall be held uncashed
      until Acceptance and then deposited within 3 business days after Acceptance
      (or ☐ _____), with Escrow Holder, (or ☐ into Broker's trust account).
   B. **INCREASED DEPOSIT:** Buyer shall deposit with Escrow Holder an increased deposit in
      the amount of . . . . $ _____
      within _____ Days After Acceptance, or ☐ _____.
   C. **FIRST LOAN IN THE AMOUNT OF** . . . . $ _____
      (1) **NEW** First Deed of Trust in favor of lender, encumbering the Property, securing a note
          payable at maximum interest of _____ % fixed rate, or _____ % initial adjustable rate
          with a maximum interest rate of _____ %, balance due in _____ years, amortized over
          _____ years. Buyer shall pay loan fees/points not to exceed _____. (These terms
          apply whether the designated loan is conventional, FHA or VA.)
      (2) ☐ **FHA** ☐ **VA:** (The following terms only apply to the FHA or VA loan that is checked.)
          Seller shall pay _____ % discount points. Seller shall pay other fees not allowed to be
          paid by Buyer, ☐ not to exceed $_____. Seller shall pay the cost of lender
          required Repairs (including those for wood destroying pest) not otherwise provided for
          in this Agreement, ☐ not to exceed $_____. (Actual loan amount may increase if
          mortgage insurance premiums, funding fees or closing costs are financed.)
   D. **ADDITIONAL FINANCING TERMS:** ☐ Seller financing (C.A.R. Form SFA); ☐ secondary . . . . $ _____
      financing (C.A.R. Form PAA, paragraph 4A); ☐ assumed financing (C.A.R. Form PAA,
      paragraph 4B) _____
      _____
      _____
   E. **BALANCE OF PURCHASE PRICE** (not including costs of obtaining loans and other closing
      costs) in the amount of . . . . $ _____
      to be deposited with Escrow Holder within sufficient time to close escrow.
   F. **PURCHASE PRICE (TOTAL):** . . . . $ _____
   G. **LOAN APPLICATIONS:** Within 7 (or ☐ _____) Days After Acceptance, Buyer shall provide Seller a letter
      from lender or mortgage loan broker stating that, based on a review of Buyer's written application and
      credit report, Buyer is prequalified or preapproved for the NEW loan specified in 2C above.
   H. **VERIFICATION OF DOWN PAYMENT AND CLOSING COSTS:** Buyer (or Buyer's lender or loan broker
      pursuant to 2G) shall, within 7 (or ☐ _____) Days After Acceptance, provide Seller written verification
      of Buyer's down payment and closing costs.

Buyer's Initials (_____)(_____)
Seller's Initials (_____)(_____)

Reviewed by _____ Date _____

NODPA 1/06 (PAGE 1 OF 10)

NOTICE OF DEFAULT PURCHASE AGREEMENT (NODPA PAGE 1 OF 10)

Property Address: _____   Date: _____

I. **LOAN CONTINGENCY REMOVAL:** (i) Within 17 (or ☐ _____) Days After Acceptance, Buyer shall, as specified in paragraph 14, remove the loan contingency or cancel this Agreement; or (ii) (if checked) ☐ the loan contingency shall remain in effect until the designated loans are funded.

J. **APPRAISAL CONTINGENCY AND REMOVAL:** This Agreement is (OR, if checked, ☐ is NOT) contingent upon the Property appraising at no less than the specified purchase price. If there is a loan contingency, at the time the loan contingency is removed (or, if checked, ☐ within 17 (or ____) Days After Acceptance), Buyer shall, as specified in paragraph 14B(3), remove the appraisal contingency or cancel this Agreement. If there is no loan contingency, Buyer shall, as specified in paragraph 14B(3), remove the appraisal contingency within 17 (or ____) Days After Acceptance.

K. ☐ **NO LOAN CONTINGENCY (If checked):** Obtaining any loan in paragraphs 2C, 2D or elsewhere in this Agreement is NOT a contingency of this Agreement. If Buyer does not obtain the loan and as a result Buyer does not purchase the Property, Seller may be entitled to Buyer's deposit or other legal remedies.

L. ☐ **ALL CASH OFFER (If checked):** No loan is needed to purchase the Property. Buyer shall, within 7 (or ☐ _____) Days After Acceptance, provide Seller written verification of sufficient funds to close this transaction.

3. **CLOSING AND OCCUPANCY:**

A. Buyer does NOT intend to occupy the Property as Buyer's primary residence.

B. Occupancy shall be delivered to Buyer at _____ AM/PM, ☐ on the date of Close Of Escrow; ☐ on _____; or ☐ no later than _____ Days After Close Of Escrow. (C.A.R. Form PAA, paragraph 2.) If transfer of title and occupancy do not occur at the same time, Buyer and Seller are advised to: (i) enter into a written occupancy agreement; and (ii) consult with their insurance and legal advisors.

C. At Close Of Escrow, Seller assigns to Buyer any assignable warranty rights for items included in the sale and shall provide any available Copies of such warranties. Brokers cannot and will not determine the assignability of any warranties.

D. At Close Of Escrow, unless otherwise agreed in writing, Seller shall provide keys and/or means to operate all locks, mailboxes, security systems, alarms and garage door openers. If Property is a condominium or located in a common interest subdivision, Buyer may be required to pay a deposit to the Homeowners' Association ("HOA") to obtain keys to accessible HOA facilities.

4. **ALLOCATION OF COSTS (If checked):** Unless otherwise specified here, this paragraph only determines who is to pay for the report, inspection, test or service mentioned. If not specified here or elsewhere in this Agreement, the determination of who is to pay for any work recommended or identified by any such report, inspection, test or service shall be by the method specified in paragraph 14B(2).

A. **WOOD DESTROYING PEST INSPECTION:**

(1) ☐ **Buyer** ☐ **Seller** shall pay for an inspection and report for wood destroying pests and organisms ("Report") which shall be prepared by _____, a registered structural pest control company. The Report shall cover the accessible areas of the main building and attached structures and, (if checked) ☐ detached garages and carports, ☐ detached decks, ☐ the following other structures or areas:_____. The Report shall not include roof coverings. If Property is a condominium or located in a common interest subdivision, the Report shall include only the separate interest and any exclusive-use areas being transferred and shall not include common areas, unless otherwise agreed. Water tests of shower pans on upper level units may not be performed without consent of the owners of property below the shower.

OR (2) ☐ (If checked) The attached addendum (C.A.R. Form WPA) regarding wood destroying pest inspection and allocation of cost is incorporated into this Agreement.

B. **OTHER INSPECTIONS AND REPORTS:**

(1) ☐ **Buyer** ☐ **Seller** shall pay to have septic or private sewage disposal systems inspected.
(2) ☐ **Buyer** ☐ **Seller** shall pay to have domestic wells tested for water potability and productivity.
(3) ☐ **Buyer** ☐ **Seller** shall pay for a natural hazard zone disclosure report prepared by: _____.
(4) ☐ **Buyer** ☐ **Seller** shall pay for the following inspection or report:_____.
(5) ☐ **Buyer** ☐ **Seller** shall pay for the following inspection or report:_____.

C. **GOVERNMENT REQUIREMENTS AND RETROFIT:**

(1) ☐ **Buyer** ☐ **Seller** shall pay for smoke detector installation and/or water heater bracing, if required by Law. Prior to Close Of Escrow, Seller shall provide Buyer a written statement of compliance in accordance with state and local Law, unless exempt.
(2) ☐ **Buyer** ☐ **Seller** shall pay the cost of compliance with any other minimum mandatory government retrofit standards, inspections and reports if required as a condition of closing escrow under any Law. _____.

Buyer's Initials (_____)(_____)
Seller's Initials (_____)(_____)
Reviewed by _____ Date _____

NODPA 1/06 (PAGE 2 OF 10)

NOTICE OF DEFAULT PURCHASE AGREEMENT (NODPA PAGE 2 OF 10)

Property Address: _____   Date: _____

    D. ESCROW AND TITLE:

      (1) ☐ Buyer ☐ Seller shall pay escrow fee _____.
          Escrow Holder shall be _____.
      (2) ☐ Buyer ☐ Seller shall pay for owner's title insurance policy specified in paragraph 12E _____
          _____.
          Owner's title policy to be issued by: _____.
          (Buyer shall pay for any title insurance policy insuring Buyer's lender, unless otherwise agreed in writing.)

    E. OTHER COSTS:

      (1) ☐ Buyer ☐ Seller shall pay County transfer tax or transfer fee _____.
      (2) ☐ Buyer ☐ Seller shall pay City transfer tax or transfer fee_____.
      (3) ☐ Buyer ☐ Seller shall pay HOA transfer fee _____.
      (4) ☐ Buyer ☐ Seller shall pay HOA document preparation fees _____.
      (5) ☐ Buyer ☐ Seller shall pay the cost, not to exceed $ _____, of a one-year home
          warranty plan, issued by _____,
          with the following optional coverage: _____.
      (6) ☐ Buyer ☐ Seller shall pay for _____.
      (7) ☐ Buyer ☐ Seller shall pay for _____.

5. **STATUTORY DISCLOSURES (INCLUDING LEAD-BASED PAINT HAZARD DISCLOSURES) AND CANCELLATION RIGHTS:**

    A. (1) Seller shall, within the time specified in paragraph 14A, deliver to Buyer, if required by Law: (i) Federal Lead-Based Paint Disclosures and pamphlet ("Lead Disclosures"); and (ii) disclosures or notices required by sections 1102 et. seq. and 1103 et. seq. of the California Civil Code ("Statutory Disclosures"). Statutory Disclosures include, but are not limited to, a Real Estate Transfer Disclosure Statement ("TDS"), Natural Hazard Disclosure Statement ("NHD"), notice or actual knowledge of release of illegal controlled substance, notice of special tax and/or assessments (or, if allowed, substantially equivalent notice regarding the Mello-Roos Community Facilities Act and Improvement Bond Act of 1915) and, if Seller has actual knowledge, an industrial use and military ordnance location disclosure (C.A.R. Form SSD).

      (2) Buyer shall, within the time specified in paragraph 14B(1), return Signed Copies of the Statutory and Lead Disclosures to Seller.

      (3) In the event Seller, prior to Close Of Escrow, becomes aware of adverse conditions materially affecting the Property, or any material inaccuracy in disclosures, information or representations previously provided to Buyer of which Buyer is otherwise unaware, Seller shall promptly provide a subsequent or amended disclosure or notice, in writing, covering those items. However, a subsequent or amended disclosure shall not be required for conditions and material inaccuracies disclosed in reports ordered and paid for by Buyer.

      (4) If any disclosure or notice specified in 5A(1), or subsequent or amended disclosure or notice is delivered to Buyer after the offer is Signed, Buyer shall have the right to cancel this Agreement within 3 Days After delivery in person, or 5 Days After delivery by deposit in the mail, by giving written notice of cancellation to Seller or Seller's agent. (Lead Disclosures sent by mail must be sent certified mail or better.)

      (5) Note to Buyer and Seller: Waiver of Statutory and Lead Disclosures is prohibited by Law.

    B. **NATURAL AND ENVIRONMENTAL HAZARDS:** Within the time specified in paragraph 14A, Seller shall, if required by Law: (i) deliver to Buyer earthquake guides (and questionnaire) and environmental hazards booklet; (ii) even if exempt from the obligation to provide a NHD, disclose if the Property is located in a Special Flood Hazard Area; Potential Flooding (Inundation) Area; Very High Fire Hazard Zone; State Fire Responsibility Area; Earthquake Fault Zone; Seismic Hazard Zone; and (iii) disclose any other zone as required by Law and provide any other information required for those zones.

    C. **MEGAN'S LAW DATABASE DISCLOSURE:** Notice: Pursuant to Section 290.46 of the Penal Code, information about specified registered sex offenders is made available to the public via an Internet Web site maintained by the Department of Justice at www.meganslaw.ca.gov. Depending on an offender's criminal history, this information will include either the address at which the offender resides or the community of residence and ZIP Code in which he or she resides. (Neither Seller nor Brokers are required to check this website. If Buyer wants further information, Broker recommends that Buyer obtain information from this website during Buyer's inspection contingency period. Brokers do not have expertise in this area.)

6. **CONDOMINIUM/PLANNED UNIT DEVELOPMENT DISCLOSURES:**

    A. **SELLER HAS:** 7 (or ☐ _____) Days After Acceptance to disclose to Buyer whether the Property is a condominium, or is located in a planned unit development or other common interest subdivision (C.A.R. Form SSD).

Buyer's Initials (_____)(_____)
Seller's Initials (_____)(_____)

Copyright © 2005-2007, CALIFORNIA ASSOCIATION OF REALTORS®, INC.
NODPA 1/06 (PAGE 3 OF 10)

Reviewed by _____ Date _____

NOTICE OF DEFAULT PURCHASE AGREEMENT (NODPA PAGE 3 OF 10)

Property Address: _____ Date: _____

B. If the Property is a condominium or is located in a planned unit development or other common interest subdivision, Seller has 3 (or ☐ _____) Days After Acceptance to request from the HOA (C.A.R. Form HOA): (i) Copies of any documents required by Law; (ii) disclosure of any pending or anticipated claim or litigation by or against the HOA; (iii) a statement containing the location and number of designated parking and storage spaces; (iv) Copies of the most recent 12 months of HOA minutes for regular and special meetings; and (v) the names and contact information of all HOAs governing the Property (collectively, "CI Disclosures"). Seller shall itemize and deliver to Buyer all CI Disclosures received from the HOA and any CI Disclosures in Seller's possession. Buyer's approval of CI Disclosures is a contingency of this Agreement as specified in paragraph 14B(3).

7. **CONDITIONS AFFECTING PROPERTY:**
   A. Unless otherwise agreed: (i) the Property is sold (a) in its **PRESENT** physical condition as of the date of Acceptance and (b) subject to Buyer's Investigation rights; (ii) the Property, including pool, spa, landscaping and grounds, is to be maintained in substantially the same condition as on the date of Acceptance; and (iii) all debris and personal property not included in the sale shall be removed by Close Of Escrow.
   B. SELLER SHALL, within the time specified in paragraph 14A, DISCLOSE KNOWN MATERIAL FACTS AND DEFECTS affecting the Property, including known insurance claims within the past five years, AND MAKE OTHER DISCLOSURES REQUIRED BY LAW (C.A.R. Form SSD).
   C. NOTE TO BUYER: You are strongly advised to conduct investigations of the entire Property in order to determine its present condition since Seller may not be aware of all defects affecting the Property or other factors that you consider important. Property improvements may not be built according to code, in compliance with current Law, or have had permits issued.
   D. NOTE TO SELLER: Buyer has the right to inspect the Property and, as specified in paragraph 14B, based upon information discovered in those inspections: (i) cancel this Agreement; or (ii) request that you make Repairs or take other action.

8. **ITEMS INCLUDED AND EXCLUDED:**
   A. NOTE TO BUYER AND SELLER: Items listed as included or excluded in the MLS, flyers or marketing materials are not included in the purchase price or excluded from the sale unless specified in 8B or C.
   B. ITEMS INCLUDED IN SALE:
      (1) All EXISTING fixtures and fittings that are attached to the Property;
      (2) Existing electrical, mechanical, lighting, plumbing and heating fixtures, ceiling fans, fireplace inserts, gas logs and grates, solar systems, built-in appliances, window and door screens, awnings, shutters, window coverings, attached floor coverings, television antennas, satellite dishes, private integrated telephone systems, air coolers/conditioners, pool/spa equipment, garage door openers/remote controls, mailbox, in-ground landscaping, trees/shrubs, water softeners, water purifiers, security systems/alarms; and
      (3) The following items: _____
      _____ .
      (4) Seller represents that all items included in the purchase price, unless otherwise specified, are owned by Seller.
      (5) All items included shall be transferred free of liens and without Seller warranty.
   C. ITEMS EXCLUDED FROM SALE: _____
      _____ .

9. **BUYER'S INVESTIGATION OF PROPERTY AND MATTERS AFFECTING PROPERTY:**
   A. Buyer's acceptance of the condition of, and any other matter affecting the Property, is a contingency of this Agreement as specified in this paragraph and paragraph 14B. Within the time specified in paragraph 14B(1), Buyer shall have the right, at Buyer's expense unless otherwise agreed, to conduct inspections, investigations, tests, surveys and other studies ("Buyer Investigations"), including, but not limited to, the right to: (i) inspect for lead-based paint and other lead-based paint hazards; (ii) inspect for wood destroying pests and organisms; (iii) review the registered sex offender database; (iv) confirm the insurability of Buyer and the Property; and (v) satisfy Buyer as to any matter specified in the attached Buyer's Inspection Advisory (C.A.R. Form BIA). Without Seller's prior written consent, Buyer shall neither make nor cause to be made: (i) invasive or destructive Buyer Investigations; or (ii) inspections by any governmental building or zoning inspector or government employee, unless required by Law.
   B. Buyer shall complete Buyer Investigations and, as specified in paragraph 14B, remove the contingency or cancel this Agreement. Buyer shall give Seller, at no cost, complete Copies of all Buyer Investigation reports obtained by Buyer. Seller shall make the Property available for all Buyer Investigations. Seller shall have water, gas, electricity and all operable pilot lights on for Buyer's Investigations and through the date possession is made available to Buyer.

Buyer's Initials (_____)(_____)
Seller's Initials (_____)(_____)

Reviewed by _____ Date _____

NOTICE OF DEFAULT PURCHASE AGREEMENT (NODPA PAGE 4 OF 10)

Property Address: _____ Date: _____

10. **REPAIRS:** Repairs shall be completed prior to final verification of condition unless otherwise agreed in writing. Repairs to be performed at Seller's expense may be performed by Seller or through others, provided that the work complies with applicable Law, including governmental permit, inspection and approval requirements. Repairs shall be performed in a good, skillful manner with materials of quality and appearance comparable to existing materials. It is understood that exact restoration of appearance or cosmetic items following all Repairs may not be possible. Seller shall: (i) obtain receipts for Repairs performed by others; (ii) prepare a written statement indicating the Repairs performed by Seller and the date of such Repairs; and (iii) provide Copies of receipts and statements to Buyer prior to final verification of condition.

11. **BUYER INDEMNITY AND SELLER PROTECTION FOR ENTRY UPON PROPERTY:** Buyer shall: (i) keep the Property free and clear of liens; (ii) Repair all damage arising from Buyer Investigations; and (iii) indemnify and hold Seller harmless from all resulting liability, claims, demands, damages and costs. Buyer shall carry, or Buyer shall require anyone acting on Buyer's behalf to carry, policies of liability, workers' compensation and other applicable insurance, defending and protecting Seller from liability for any injuries to persons or property occurring during any Buyer Investigations or work done on the Property at Buyer's direction prior to Close Of Escrow. Seller is advised that certain protections may be afforded Seller by recording a "Notice of Non-responsibility" (C.A.R. Form NNR) for Buyer Investigations and work done on the Property at Buyer's direction. Buyer's obligations under this paragraph shall survive the termination of this Agreement.

12. **TITLE AND VESTING:**
    A. Within the time specified in paragraph 14, Buyer shall be provided a current preliminary (title) report, which is only an offer by the title insurer to issue a policy of title insurance and may not contain every item affecting title. Buyer's review of the preliminary report and any other matters which may affect title are a contingency of this Agreement as specified in paragraph 14B.
    B. Title is taken in its present condition subject to all encumbrances, easements, covenants, conditions, restrictions, rights and other matters, whether of record or not, as of the date of Acceptance except: (i) monetary liens of record unless Buyer is assuming those obligations or taking the Property subject to those obligations; and (ii) those matters which Seller has agreed to remove in writing.
    C. Within the time specified in paragraph 14A, Seller has a duty to disclose to Buyer all matters known to Seller affecting title, whether of record or not.
    D. At Close Of Escrow, Buyer shall receive a grant deed conveying title (or, for stock cooperative or long-term lease, an assignment of stock certificate or of Seller's leasehold interest), including oil, mineral and water rights if currently owned by Seller. Title shall vest as designated in Buyer's supplemental escrow instructions. THE MANNER OF TAKING TITLE MAY HAVE SIGNIFICANT LEGAL AND TAX CONSEQUENCES. CONSULT AN APPROPRIATE PROFESSIONAL.
    E. Buyer shall receive a CLTA/ALTA Homeowner's Policy of Title Insurance. A title company, at Buyer's request, can provide information about the availability, desirability, coverage, and cost of various title insurance coverages and endorsements. If Buyer desires title coverage other than that required by this paragraph, Buyer shall instruct Escrow Holder in writing and pay any increase in cost.

13. **SALE OF BUYER'S PROPERTY:**
    A. This Agreement is NOT contingent upon the sale of any property owned by Buyer.
    OR B. ☐ (If checked): The attached addendum (C.A.R. Form COP) regarding the contingency for the sale of property owned by Buyer is incorporated into this Agreement.

14. **TIME PERIODS; REMOVAL OF CONTINGENCIES; CANCELLATION RIGHTS:** The following time periods may only be extended, altered, modified or changed by mutual written agreement. Any removal of contingencies or cancellation under this paragraph must be in writing (C.A.R. Form CR).
    A. **SELLER HAS: 7 (or ☐ _____) Days After Acceptance** to deliver to Buyer all reports, disclosures and information for which Seller is responsible under paragraphs 4, 5A and B, 6A, 7B, and 12.
    B. (1) **BUYER HAS: 17 (or ☐ _____) Days After Acceptance,** unless otherwise agreed in writing, to: (i) complete all Buyer Investigations; approve all disclosures, reports and other applicable information, which Buyer receives from Seller; and approve all matters affecting the Property (including lead-based paint and lead-based paint hazards as well as other information specified in paragraph 5 and insurability of Buyer and the Property); and (ii) return to Seller Signed Copies of Statutory and Lead Disclosures delivered by Seller in accordance with paragraph 5A.
    (2) Within the time specified in 14B(1), Buyer may request that Seller make repairs or take any other action regarding the Property (C.A.R. Form RR). Seller has no obligation to agree to or respond to Buyer's requests.

Buyer's Initials (_____)(_____)
Seller's Initials (_____)(_____)

NODPA 1/06 (PAGE 5 OF 10)

Reviewed by _____ Date _____

NOTICE OF DEFAULT PURCHASE AGREEMENT (NODPA PAGE 5 OF 10)

Property Address: _____ Date: _____

(3) By the end of the time specified in 14B(1) (or 2I for loan contingency or 2J for appraisal contingency), Buyer shall, in writing, remove the applicable contingency (C.A.R. Form CR) or cancel this Agreement. However, if (i) government-mandated inspections/ reports required as a condition of closing; or (ii) Common Interest Disclosures pursuant to paragraph 6B are not made within the time specified in 14A, then Buyer has 5 (or ☐ _____) Days After receipt of any such items, or the time specified in 14B(1), whichever is later, to remove the applicable contingency or cancel this Agreement in writing.

C. **CONTINUATION OF CONTINGENCY OR CONTRACTUAL OBLIGATION; SELLER RIGHT TO CANCEL:**

(1) Seller right to Cancel; Buyer Contingencies: Seller, after first giving Buyer a Notice to Buyer to Perform (as specified below), may cancel this Agreement in writing and authorize return of Buyer's deposit if, by the time specified in this Agreement, Buyer does not remove in writing the applicable contingency or cancel this Agreement. Once all contingencies have been removed, failure of either Buyer or Seller to close escrow on time may be a breach of this Agreement.

(2) Continuation of Contingency: Even after the expiration of the time specified in 14B, Buyer retains the right to make requests to Seller, remove in writing the applicable contingency or cancel this Agreement until Seller cancels pursuant to 14C(1). Once Seller receives Buyer's written removal of all contingencies, Seller may not cancel this Agreement pursuant to 14C(1).

(3) Seller right to Cancel; Buyer Contract Obligations: Seller, after first giving Buyer a Notice to Buyer to Perform (as specified below), may cancel this Agreement in writing and authorize return of Buyer's deposit for any of the following reasons: (i) if Buyer fails to deposit funds as required by 2A or 2B; (ii) if the funds deposited pursuant to 2A or 2B are not good when deposited; (iii) if Buyer fails to provide a letter as required by 2G; (iv) if Buyer fails to provide verification as required by 2H or 2L; (v) if Seller reasonably disapproves of the verification provided by 2H or 2L; (vi) if Buyer fails to return Statutory and Lead Disclosures as required by paragraph 5A(2); or (vii) if Buyer fails to sign or initial a separate liquidated damage form for an increased deposit as required by paragraph 16. Seller is not required to give Buyer a Notice to Perform regarding Close of Escrow.

(4) Notice To Buyer To Perform: The Notice to Buyer to Perform (C.A.R. Form NBP) shall: (i) be in writing; (ii) be signed by Seller; and (iii) give Buyer at least 24 (or ☐ _____) hours (or until the time specified in the applicable paragraph, whichever occurs last) to take the applicable action. A Notice to Buyer to Perform may not be given any earlier than 2 Days Prior to the expiration of the applicable time for Buyer to remove a contingency or cancel this Agreement or meet a 14C(3) obligation.

D. **EFFECT OF BUYER'S REMOVAL OF CONTINGENCIES:** If Buyer removes, in writing, any contingency or cancellation rights, unless otherwise specified in a separate written agreement between Buyer and Seller, Buyer shall conclusively be deemed to have: (i) completed all Buyer Investigations, and review of reports and other applicable information and disclosures pertaining to that contingency or cancellation right; (ii) elected to proceed with the transaction; and (iii) assumed all liability, responsibility and expense for repairs or corrections pertaining to that contingency or cancellation right, or for inability to obtain financing.

E. **EFFECT OF CANCELLATION ON DEPOSITS:** If Buyer or Seller gives written notice of cancellation pursuant to rights duly exercised under the terms of this Agreement, Buyer and Seller agree to Sign mutual instructions to cancel the sale and escrow and release deposits to the party entitled to the funds, less fees and costs incurred by that party. Fees and costs may be payable to service providers and vendors for services and products provided during escrow. Release of funds will require mutual Signed release instructions from Buyer and Seller, judicial decision or arbitration award. A party may be subject to a civil penalty of up to $1,000 for refusal to sign such instructions if no good faith dispute exists as to who is entitled to the deposited funds (Civil Code §1057.3).

15. **FINAL VERIFICATION OF CONDITION:** Buyer shall have the right to make a final inspection of the Property within 5 (or _____) Days Prior to Close Of Escrow, NOT AS A CONTINGENCY OF THE SALE, but solely to confirm: (i) the Property is maintained pursuant to paragraph 7A; (ii) Repairs have been completed as agreed; and (iii) Seller has complied with Seller's other obligations under this Agreement.

16. **LIQUIDATED DAMAGES:** If Buyer fails to complete this purchase because of Buyer's default, Seller shall retain, as liquidated damages, the deposit actually paid. If the Property is a dwelling with no more than four units, one of which Buyer intends to occupy, then the amount retained shall be no more than 3% of the purchase price. Any excess shall be returned to Buyer. Release of funds will require mutual, Signed release instructions from both Buyer and Seller, judicial decision or arbitration award.
BUYER AND SELLER SHALL SIGN A SEPARATE LIQUIDATED DAMAGES PROVISION FOR ANY INCREASED DEPOSIT (C.A.R. FORM RID).

Buyer's Initials _____/_____	Seller's Initials _____/_____

NODPA 1/06 (PAGE 6 OF 10)

Buyer's Initials (_____)(_____)
Seller's Initials (_____)(_____)

Reviewed by _____ Date _____

EQUAL HOUSING OPPORTUNITY

NOTICE OF DEFAULT PURCHASE AGREEMENT (NODPA PAGE 6 OF 10)

Property Address: _____   Date: _____

17. DISPUTE RESOLUTION:

  A. **MEDIATION:** Buyer and Seller agree to mediate any dispute or claim arising between them out of this Agreement, or any resulting transaction, before resorting to arbitration or court action. Paragraphs 17B(2) and (3) below apply to mediation whether or not the Arbitration provision is initialed. Mediation fees, if any, shall be divided equally among the parties involved. If, for any dispute or claim to which this paragraph applies, any party commences an action without first attempting to resolve the matter through mediation, or refuses to mediate after a request has been made, then that party shall not be entitled to recover attorney fees, even if they would otherwise be available to that party in any such action. THIS MEDIATION PROVISION APPLIES WHETHER OR NOT THE ARBITRATION PROVISION IS INITIALED.

  B. **ARBITRATION OF DISPUTES:** (1) Buyer and Seller agree that any dispute or claim in Law or equity arising between them out of this Agreement or any resulting transaction, which is not settled through mediation, shall be decided by neutral, binding arbitration, including and subject to paragraphs 17B(2) and (3) below. The arbitrator shall be a retired judge or justice, or an attorney with at least 5 years of residential real estate Law experience, unless the parties mutually agree to a different arbitrator, who shall render an award in accordance with substantive California Law. The parties shall have the right to discovery in accordance with California Code of Civil Procedure § 1283.05. In all other respects, the arbitration shall be conducted in accordance with Title 9 of Part III of the California Code of Civil Procedure. Judgment upon the award of the arbitrator(s) may be entered into any court having jurisdiction. Interpretation of this Agreement to arbitrate shall be governed by the Federal Arbitration Act.

  (2) **EXCLUSIONS FROM MEDIATION AND ARBITRATION:** The following matters are excluded from mediation and arbitration: (i) a judicial or non-judicial foreclosure or other action or proceeding to enforce a deed of trust, mortgage or installment land sale contract as defined in California Civil Code § 2985; (ii) an unlawful detainer action; (iii) the filing or enforcement of a mechanic's lien; and (iv) any matter that is within the jurisdiction of a probate, small claims or bankruptcy court. The filing of a court action to enable the recording of a notice of pending action, for order of attachment, receivership, injunction, or other provisional remedies, shall not constitute a waiver of the mediation and arbitration provisions.

  (3) **BROKERS:** Buyer and Seller agree to mediate and arbitrate disputes or claims involving either or both Brokers, consistent with 17A and B, provided either or both Brokers shall have agreed to such mediation or arbitration prior to, or within a reasonable time after, the dispute or claim is presented to Brokers. Any election by either or both Brokers to participate in mediation or arbitration shall not result in Brokers being deemed parties to the Agreement.

  "NOTICE: BY INITIALING IN THE SPACE BELOW YOU ARE AGREEING TO HAVE ANY DISPUTE ARISING OUT OF THE MATTERS INCLUDED IN THE 'ARBITRATION OF DISPUTES' PROVISION DECIDED BY NEUTRAL ARBITRATION AS PROVIDED BY CALIFORNIA LAW AND YOU ARE GIVING UP ANY RIGHTS YOU MIGHT POSSESS TO HAVE THE DISPUTE LITIGATED IN A COURT OR JURY TRIAL. BY INITIALING IN THE SPACE BELOW YOU ARE GIVING UP YOUR JUDICIAL RIGHTS TO DISCOVERY AND APPEAL, UNLESS THOSE RIGHTS ARE SPECIFICALLY INCLUDED IN THE 'ARBITRATION OF DISPUTES' PROVISION. IF YOU REFUSE TO SUBMIT TO ARBITRATION AFTER AGREEING TO THIS PROVISION, YOU MAY BE COMPELLED TO ARBITRATE UNDER THE AUTHORITY OF THE CALIFORNIA CODE OF CIVIL PROCEDURE. YOUR AGREEMENT TO THIS ARBITRATION PROVISION IS VOLUNTARY."

  "WE HAVE READ AND UNDERSTAND THE FOREGOING AND AGREE TO SUBMIT DISPUTES ARISING OUT OF THE MATTERS INCLUDED IN THE 'ARBITRATION OF DISPUTES' PROVISION TO NEUTRAL ARBITRATION."

Buyer's Initials _____/_____	Seller's Initials _____/_____

18. PRORATIONS OF PROPERTY TAXES AND OTHER ITEMS: Unless otherwise agreed in writing, the following items shall be PAID CURRENT and prorated between Buyer and Seller as of Close Of Escrow: real property taxes and assessments, interest, rents, HOA regular, special and emergency dues and assessments imposed prior to Close Of Escrow, premiums on insurance assumed by Buyer, payments on bonds and assessments assumed by Buyer, and payments on Mello-Roos and other Special Assessment District bonds and assessments that are now a lien. The following items shall be assumed by Buyer WITHOUT CREDIT toward the purchase price: prorated payments on Mello-Roos and other Special Assessment District bonds and assessments and HOA special assessments that are now a lien but not yet due. Property will be reassessed upon change of ownership. Any supplemental tax bills shall be paid as follows: (i) for periods after Close Of Escrow, by Buyer; and (ii) for periods prior to Close Of Escrow, by Seller. TAX BILLS ISSUED AFTER CLOSE OF ESCROW SHALL BE HANDLED DIRECTLY BETWEEN BUYER AND SELLER. Prorations shall be made based on a 30-day month.

Buyer's Initials (_____)(_____)
Seller's Initials (_____)(_____)

NODPA 1/06 (PAGE 7 OF 10)

Reviewed by _____ Date _____

NOTICE OF DEFAULT PURCHASE AGREEMENT (NODPA PAGE 7 OF 10)

Property Address: _____ Date: _____

19. **WITHHOLDING TAXES:** Seller and Buyer agree to execute any instrument, affidavit, statement or instruction reasonably necessary to comply with federal (FIRPTA) and California withholding Law, if required (C.A.R. Form AS).

20. **MULTIPLE LISTING SERVICE ("MLS"):** Brokers are authorized to report to the MLS a pending sale and, upon Close Of Escrow, the terms of this transaction to be published and disseminated to persons and entities authorized to use the information on terms approved by the MLS.

21. **EQUAL HOUSING OPPORTUNITY:** The Property is sold in compliance with federal, state and local anti-discrimination Laws.

22. **ATTORNEY FEES:** In any action, proceeding or arbitration between Buyer and Seller arising out of this Agreement, the prevailing Buyer or Seller shall be entitled to reasonable attorney fees and costs from the non-prevailing Buyer or Seller, except as provided in paragraph 17A.

23. **SELECTION OF SERVICE PROVIDERS:** If Brokers refer Buyer or Seller to persons, vendors, or service or product providers ("Providers"), Brokers do not guarantee the performance of any Providers. Buyer and Seller may select ANY Providers of their own choosing.

24. **TIME OF ESSENCE; ENTIRE CONTRACT; CHANGES:** Time is of the essence. All understandings between the parties are incorporated in this Agreement. Its terms are intended by the parties as a final, complete and exclusive expression of their Agreement with respect to its subject matter, and may not be contradicted by evidence of any prior agreement or contemporaneous oral agreement. If any provision of this Agreement is held to be ineffective or invalid, the remaining provisions will nevertheless be given full force and effect. Neither this Agreement nor any provision in it may be extended, amended, modified, altered or changed, except in writing Signed by Buyer and Seller.

25. **OTHER TERMS AND CONDITIONS, including attached supplements:**
    A. ☑ Buyer's Inspection Advisory (C.A.R. Form BIA) _____
    B. ☐ Purchase Agreement Addendum (C.A.R. Form PAA paragraph numbers: _____)
    C. ☐ Statewide Buyer and Seller Advisory (C.A.R. Form SBSA) _____
    D. _____
       _____
       _____

26. **DEFINITIONS:** As used in this Agreement:
    A. "Acceptance" means the time the offer or final counter offer is accepted in writing by a party and is delivered to and personally received by the other party or that party's authorized agent in accordance with the terms of this offer or a final counter offer.
    B. "Agreement" means the terms and conditions of this accepted California Residential Purchase Agreement and any accepted counter offers and addenda.
    C. "C.A.R. Form" means the specific form referenced or another comparable form agreed to by the parties.
    D. "Close Of Escrow" means the date the grant deed, or other evidence of transfer of title, is recorded. If the scheduled Close Of Escrow falls on a Saturday, Sunday or legal holiday, then Close Of Escrow shall be the next business Day After the scheduled Close Of Escrow date.
    E. "Copy" means copy by any means including photocopy, NCR, facsimile and electronic.
    F. "Days" means calendar Days, unless otherwise required by Law.
    G. "Days After" means the specified number of calendar Days After the occurrence of the event specified, not counting the calendar date on which the specified event occurs, and ending at 11:59PM on the final Day.
    H. "Days Prior" means the specified number of calendar Days before the occurrence of the event specified, not counting the calendar date on which the specified event is scheduled to occur.
    I. "Electronic Copy" or "Electronic Signature" means, as applicable, an electronic copy or signature complying with California Law. Buyer and Seller agree that electronic means will not be used by either party to modify or alter the content or integrity of this Agreement without the knowledge and consent of the other.
    J. "Law" means any Law, code, statute, ordinance, regulation, rule or order, which is adopted by a controlling city, county, state or federal legislative, judicial or executive body or agency.
    K. "Notice to Buyer to Perform" means a document (C.A.R. Form NBP), which shall be in writing and Signed by Seller and shall give Buyer at least 24 hours (or as otherwise specified in paragraph 14C(4)) to remove a contingency or perform as applicable.
    L. "Repairs" means any repairs (including pest control), alterations, replacements, modifications or retrofitting of the Property provided for under this Agreement.
    M. "Signed" means either a handwritten or electronic signature on an original document, Copy or any counterpart.
    N. Singular and Plural terms each include the other, when appropriate.

Buyer's Initials (_____)(_____)
Seller's Initials (_____)(_____)

NODPA 1/06 (PAGE 8 OF 10)

| Reviewed by _____ Date _____ |

EQUAL HOUSING OPPORTUNITY

NOTICE OF DEFAULT PURCHASE AGREEMENT (NODPA PAGE 8 OF 10)

Property Address: _____ Date: _____

27. JOINT ESCROW INSTRUCTIONS TO ESCROW HOLDER:

  A. The following paragraphs, or applicable portions thereof, of this Agreement constitute the joint escrow instructions of Buyer and Seller to Escrow Holder, which Escrow Holder is to use along with any related counter offers and addenda, and any additional mutual instructions to Close The Escrow: 1, 2, 4, 12, 13B, 14E, 18, 19, 24, 25B and D, 26, 27, 30A and 31. If a Copy of the separate compensation agreement provided for in paragraph 30A, is deposited with Escrow Holder by Broker, Escrow Holder shall accept such agreement and pay out from Buyer's or Seller's funds, OR BOTH, AS APPLICABLE, the Broker's compensation provided for in such agreement(s). The terms and conditions of this Agreement not set forth in the specified paragraphs are additional matters for the information of Escrow Holder, but about which Escrow Holder need not be concerned. Buyer and Seller will receive Escrow Holder's general provisions directly from Escrow Holder and will execute such provisions upon Escrow Holder's request. To the extent the general provisions are inconsistent or conflict with this Agreement, the general provisions will control as to the duties and obligations of Escrow Holder only. Buyer and Seller will execute additional instructions, documents and forms provided by Escrow Holder that are reasonably necessary to close the escrow.

  B. A Copy of this Agreement shall be delivered to Escrow Holder within 3 business Days After Acceptance (or ☐ _____). Buyer and Seller authorize Escrow Holder to accept and rely on Copies and Signatures as defined in this Agreement as originals, to open escrow and for other purposes of escrow. The validity of this Agreement as between Buyer and Seller is not affected by whether or when Escrow Holder Signs this Agreement.

  C. Brokers are a party to the escrow for the sole purpose of compensation pursuant to paragraph 30A. Seller irrevocably assigns to Brokers compensation specified in paragraph 30A and irrevocably instruct Escrow Holder to disburse those funds to Brokers at Close Of Escrow or pursuant to any other mutually executed cancellation agreement. Compensation instructions can be amended or revoked only with the written consent of Brokers. Escrow Holder shall immediately notify Brokers: (i) if Buyer's initial or any additional deposit is not made pursuant to this Agreement, or is not good at time of deposit with Escrow Holder; or (ii) if Buyer and Seller instruct Escrow Holder to cancel escrow.

  D. A Copy of any amendment that affects any paragraph of this Agreement for which Escrow Holder is responsible shall be delivered to Escrow Holder within 2 business Days After mutual execution of the amendment.

28. TERMS AND CONDITIONS OF OFFER:

This is an offer to purchase the Property on the above terms and conditions. All paragraphs with spaces for initials by Buyer and Seller are incorporated in this Agreement only if initialed by all parties. If at least one but not all parties initial, a counter offer is required until agreement is reached. Seller has the right to continue to offer the Property for sale and to accept any other offer at any time prior to notification of Acceptance. Buyer has read and acknowledges receipt of a Copy of the offer and agrees to the above confirmation of agency relationships. If this offer is accepted and Buyer subsequently defaults, Buyer may be responsible for payment of Brokers' compensation. This Agreement and any supplement, addendum or modification, including any Copy, may be Signed in two or more counterparts, all of which shall constitute one and the same writing.

29. EXPIRATION OF OFFER: This offer shall be deemed revoked and the deposit shall be returned unless the offer is Signed by Seller and a Copy of the Signed offer is personally received by Buyer, or by _____, who is authorized to receive it by 5:00 p.m. on the third Day after this offer is signed by Buyer (or, if checked, ☐ by _____ (date), at _____ AM/PM).

Buyer _____ Date _____

(Print name)

Buyer _____ Date _____

(Print name)

Address _____ City _____ State _____ Zip _____

Telephone _____ Fax _____ E-mail _____

30. BROKER COMPENSATION FROM SELLER:

  A. Upon Close Of Escrow, Seller agrees to pay compensation to Broker as specified in a separate written agreement between Seller and Broker.

  B. If escrow does not close, compensation is payable as specified in that separate written agreement.

Buyer's Initials (_____)(_____)
Seller's Initials (_____)(_____)

NODPA 1/06 (PAGE 9 OF 10)

Reviewed by _____ Date _____

NOTICE OF DEFAULT PURCHASE AGREEMENT (NODPA PAGE 9 OF 10)

Property Address: _____ Date: _____

31. **ACCEPTANCE OF OFFER:** Seller warrants that Seller is the owner of the Property, or has the authority to execute this Agreement. Seller accepts the above offer, agrees to sell the Property on the above terms and conditions. Seller has read and acknowledges receipt of a Copy of this Agreement and authorizes Broker to deliver a Signed Copy to Buyer.
☐ **(If checked) SUBJECT TO ATTACHED COUNTER OFFER, DATED** _____.

NOTICE REQUIRED BY CALIFORNIA LAW

UNTIL YOUR RIGHT TO CANCEL THIS CONTRACT HAS ENDED, _____ **(BUYER'S NAME)**
OR ANYONE WORKING FOR _____
(BUYER'S NAME) CANNOT ASK YOU TO SIGN OR HAVE YOU SIGN ANY DEED OR ANY OTHER DOCUMENT.

You may cancel this contract for the sale of your house without any penalty or obligation at any time before midnight on _____.
(Enter date five business days after date of contract) or 8 a.m. on _____ (the day of the scheduled foreclosure sale) whichever occurs first.
See the attached notice of cancellation form for an explanation of this right.

Seller _____ Date _____

(Print name)
Address_____ City _____ State _____ Zip _____

Seller _____ Date _____

(Print name)
Address_____ City _____ State _____ Zip _____

(____/____) **CONFIRMATION OF ACCEPTANCE:** A Copy of Signed Acceptance was personally received by Buyer
(Initials) on (date) _____ at _____ AM/PM. Completion of this confirmation is not legally required in order to create a binding Agreement; it is solely intended to evidence the date that Confirmation of Acceptance has occurred.

(____/____) **REJECTION OF OFFER:** No counter offer is being made. This offer was reviewed and rejected by
(Seller's Initials) **Seller on (Date)** _____.

ESCROW HOLDER ACKNOWLEDGMENT:
Escrow Holder acknowledges receipt of a Copy of this Agreement, (if checked, ☐ a deposit in the amount of $ _____
_____), counter offer numbers _____ and _____,
and agrees to act as Escrow Holder subject to paragraph 27 of this Agreement, any supplemental escrow instructions and the terms of Escrow Holder's general provisions.

Escrow Holder is advised that the date of Confirmation of Acceptance of the Agreement as between Buyer and Seller is
_____

Escrow Holder _____ **Escrow #** _____
By _____ **Date** _____
Address _____ **City** _____ **State** _____ **Zip** _____
Telephone _____ **Fax** _____ **E-mail** _____
Escrow Holder is licensed by the California Department of ☐ Corporations, ☐ Insurance, ☐ Real Estate.
License # _____

Published and Distributed by:
REAL ESTATE BUSINESS SERVICES, INC.
a subsidiary of the California Association of REALTORS®
525 South Virgil Avenue, Los Angeles, California 90020

NODPA 1/06 (PAGE 10 OF 10)

Reviewed by _____ Date _____

NOTICE OF DEFAULT PURCHASE AGREEMENT (NODPA PAGE 10 OF 10)

NOTICE OF CANCELLATION OF
NOTICE OF DEFAULT PURCHASE AGREEMENT

_____
(Enter date of contract)

You may cancel this contract for the sale of your house, without any penalty or obligation, at any time before _____ (Enter date and time of day).

To cancel this transaction, personally deliver a signed and dated copy of this cancellation notice, or send a telegram to _____ (Name of purchaser), at _____ (Street address of purchaser's place of business) NOT LATER THAN _____ (Enter date and time of day).

I hereby cancel this transaction _____ (Date)
_____ (Seller's signature)

Note: Except for Seller's signature and date, this Notice to be completed by Buyer prior to presenting the Agreement to Seller. Civil Code § 1695.5(b)

NOTICE OF CANCELLATION OF
NOTICE OF DEFAULT PURCHASE AGREEMENT

_____
(Enter date of contract)

You may cancel this contract for the sale of your house, without any penalty or obligation, at any time before _____ (Enter date and time of day).

To cancel this transaction, personally deliver a signed and dated copy of this cancellation notice, or send a telegram to _____ (Name of purchaser), at _____ (Street address of purchaser's place of business) NOT LATER THAN _____ (Enter date and time of day).

I hereby cancel this transaction _____ (Date)
_____ (Seller's signature)

Note: Except for Seller's signature and date, this Notice to be completed by Buyer prior to presenting the Agreement to Seller. Civil Code § 1695.5(b)

R E B S / I N C ®

Published and Distributed by:
REAL ESTATE BUSINESS SERVICES, INC.
a subsidiary of the California Association of REALTORS®
525 South Virgil Avenue, Los Angeles, California 90020

HENC 1/06 (PAGE 1 OF 1)

Reviewed by _____ Date _____

EQUAL HOUSING OPPORTUNITY

NOTICE OF CANCELLATION OF NOTICE OF DEFAULT PURCHASE AGREEMENT (HENC PAGE 1 OF 1)

Glossary

ABSTRACT OF JUDGMENT: Summary of a Court's order. When recorded, it creates a general lien upon real and personal property of a judgment debtor in the county where recorded.

ABUTTING: Land that touches or borders the land of another.

ACCELERATION CLAUSE: Provision in a trust deed or mortgage which makes the balance owed immediately due and payable upon the happening of a certain event.

ACCEPTANCE: Consent to an offer to ender into a contract.

ACCRUED DEPRECIATION: A formal declaration before an authorized official (usually a notary public) by a person who has executed a document that he, in fact, did execute (sign) the document.

ACRE: A measure of land equaling 43, 560 square feet of land area. (A square acre is approximately 209' x 209'.)

ACTION TO QUIET TITLE: A court auction to remove any interest or claim in or to the title to real property.

ADMINISTRATOR: Person appointed by the probate court to administrator the estate of a deceased person.

AFFIDAVIT: A written statement of facts sworn to or affirmed by oath before an authorized official (usually a notary public)

ALIENATE: To transfer the title to real property from on person to anther.

ALIENATION CLAUSE: A special type of acceleration clause which demands payment of the entire loan balance upon sale or other transfer of the title.

ATLA TITLE POLICY: A broad form title insurance policy issued to lenders. American Land Title Association.

AMORTIZED LOAN: A loan in which the principal payments are paid in installments.

APPRAISAL: Estimate or opinion of value.

APPRECIATION: Increase in value due to any cause.

APPURTENANCE: Anything incident to or attached to the land which is part of the property.

ASSESSED VALUE: Value placed on property for the purpose of computing real property taxes.

ASSESSOR: Official who determines assessed value for tax purposes.

ASSIGN: To transfer over to another a claim right or title to property.

ASSIGNMENT OF RENTS CLAUSE: A clause in a trust deed which gives the beneficiary the right to collect rents of the secured property in the event of a default.

ASSUPTION OF MORTGAGE (or Trust Deed): Taking over the primary liability for payment of an existing mortgage or trust deed.

ATTACHMENT: Seizure of property by court order, usually done to have it available to perform certain acts for another.

BALLOON PAYMENT: The final payment on a note which is greater than the preceding installment payments. The real estate law considers any final payment that is twice as great as the smallest installment payment as a balloon payment.

BENEFICIARY: One who receives the income from a trustor. The lender on a note and trust deed transaction.

BENEFICIARY'S STATEMENT: Statement of a lender, giving the remaining principal balance and other information concerning the loan. Usually obtained when an owner wishes to sell or refinance. Referred to as a "Bene Statement" or "Offset Statement."

BILL OF SALE: Document used to transfer title (ownership) of personal property.

BLANKET MORTGAGE (or Trust Deed): A mortgage or trust deed which covers more than one lot of parcel of real estate.

BLIND ADVERTISING: Failure by licensee to indicate license status in any advertising which pertains to real estate activity or service.
BONA FIDE: In good faith, without fraud.

BROKER: A natural or legal person who, for compensation or in expectation of compensation, acts for another in a real estate or related transaction.

CAPITALIZATION: In appraising, determining value of property by consider net income and percentage of reasonable return on the investment.

CASH FLOW: The spendable income from an investment, after deducting from gross   income all operating expenses, loan payments, and an allowance for the income tax attribute to the income.

CHAIN OF TITLE: A history of all the documents transferring title to a parcel of real estate, beginning with the document originally transferring title from the government to private ownership, and ending with the latest document transferring title.

CHATTEL MORTGAGE: A personal property mortgage.

CLOSING STATEMENT: A financial statement rendered to the buyer and seller at the close of escrow giving an account of all funds received or expended by the escrow holder.

CLOUD ON THE TITLE: Any condition which affects the clear title to real property.

COMMITMENT: An agreement to loan money.
        FHA-FIRM: An agreement by FHA to insure a loan on a specified property with a specified borrower.
        FHA-CONDITIONAL: A tentative commitment subject to the approval of an unknown borrower.

COMMUNITY PROPERTY: Property accumulated through the joint efforts or a husband and wife living together.

COMPARATIVE ANALYSIS: A method of appraisal in which selling prices of similar properties are used as the basis for arriving at the value estimate. Also know as Market Data Approach.

COMPENSATION: Money or equivalent in money received for services.

CONDEMNATION: The act of taking private property—through the exercise of the power of eminent domain—for public use, upon the payment of a fair compensation.

CONDITION: A stipulation or qualification in a deed which, if violated or not performed, defeats the deed and places the title back in the hands of the original grantor. Also may mean a requirement before the performances or completion of effectiveness of something else.

CONDITIONAL SALES CONTRACT: A contract for the sale of real or personal property in which possession of a parcel of real property, together with separate interest in space in a residential, industrial, or commercial building.

CONDOMINIUM: An estate in real property consisting of an undivided interest in common in a portion of a parcel of real property, together with separate interest in space in a residential, industrial, or commercial building

CONSIDERATION: Anything of value to induce another to enter into a contract. It may be money, services, a promise, or love and affection.

CONTINGENCY: A condition upon which a valid contract is dependent.

CONTRACT: An agreement to do or not to do a certain thing.

CONVENTIONAL FINANCING: Any loan made without government participation.

CONVEY: To transfer title to property from one person to another.

CONVEYANCE: A document, such as a deed, used to transfer title to property from one person to another.

CORPORATION: An artificial "person" created by law which has many powers and duties of an individual.

COST APPROACH: An appraisal technique used to established value by estimating the cost to reproduce the improvements, allowing for depreciation.

DBA: Abbreviation for "Doing Business As."

DEDICATION: An appropriation of land by its owner for public use has been accepted for such use by authorized public officials on behalf of the public.

DEED: Written instrument which, when properly executed and delivered, transfers title to real estate.

DEED OF RECONVEYANCE: The transfer of legal title from the trustee to the trustor (borrower) after a trust deed debt has been paid.

DEFAULT: Failure to perform a duty or to discharge an obligation.

DEFICIENCY JUDGMENT: A court order to pay the balance (deficiency) owed on a loan after the proceeds from sale of the security are not sufficient to pay off the loan.

DEMAND: One of the four essential elements of value.

DEPARTMENT OF VETERANS AFFAIRS: The state agency which administers the California Veterans Farm and Home Purchase Plan (Cal-Vet loans).

DEPOSIT RECEIPT: A form used to accept "earnest money" to bind an offer for the purchase of real property.

DEPRECIATION: Loss in value due to any cause.

DETERIORATION: Loss in value due to wear and tear.

DISCOUNT: To sell a note for less than its face value. To receive the present value of a note, minus a deduction to cover interest.

DISCOUNT POINTS: A loan fee charged by a lender when accepting an FHA or G.I. loan, to offset the lower interest received in comparison with conventional loan interest rates.

DOCUMENTARY TRANSFER TAX: A method of taxing real property transfers. Most California counties require that a tax be paid prior to recording the deed @ $1.10 per $1,000 of equity.

EASEMENT: A right to use the land of another.

ECONOMIC LIFE: The period during which an improvement earns enough profit to justify maintaining it.

ECONOMIC OBSOLESCENCE: Loss in value due to reduced desirability and usefulness of a structure due to extraneous cases, i.e., zoning, regulations, deteriorating neighborhood. Also called social obsolescence.

ECONOMIC RENT: The amount of rent which the space would bring in the open market at the time of the appraisal

EFFECTIVE AGE: The age assigned to the improvements by the appraiser which in his judgment reflects the true age of the improvement and not necessarily the chronological age.

EMINENT DOMAIN: The power of the government to take (condemn) private property for a public use up on payment of fair compensation.

ENCUMBER: Anything which burdens (limits) the free title to property such as a lien, easement, or restriction of any kind.

ENDORSEMENT: Signature on the back of a promissory note or check for the purpose of transferring ownership.
    "In Blank": Guarantees payment to subsequent holders.
    "Without Recourse": Does not guarantee payment to subsequent holders.

EQUITY: The value of real estate over and above the liens against it. It is obtained by subtracting the total liens from the value.

EQUITY PURCHASE: Buying that amount obtained by subtracting liens from value.

ESCHEAT: Reverting of property to the State upon death of an owner without heirs.

ESCROW: A transaction, usually a sale, wherein one person delivers evidence of title to a third person to be held by such third person until the happening of the performance of a prescribed condition, when the evidence of title is then delivered to the buyer.

ESCROW HOLDER: A third party, usually a corporation, who acts as the stakes holder for a buyer and seller. Escrow holder acts as an agent for buyer and seller.

ESTATE: The ownership interest of a person in real property. Also used to refer to the property left by a deceased person.

EXCLUSIVE AGENCY LISTING: A written instrument giving one agent the right to sell property for a specified period of time, but reserving the right of owner to sell the property himself without the payment of a commission.

EXCLUSIVE RIGHT TO SELL LISTING: A written agreement between owner and agent giving the agent the right to collect a commission if the property is sold by anyone during the term of his agreement.

EXECUTE: To complete, to make, to perform, to do, to follow out; to execute a deed, including especially signing, sealing, and delivering; to execute a contract is to perform the contract, to follow out to the end, to complete.

EXECUTED: A contract that has been fully performed; to sign an instrument.

FEDERAL HOUSING ADMINISTRATION (FHA): The federal government agency which administers FHA insured loans.

FEE SIMPLE ABSOLUTE ESTATE: Ownership of title to real property without limitation or end; in perpetuity. The greatest and most inclusive type of real estate ownership.

FIDUCIARY: A person holding a position of trust. Agents, trustees, executors, administrators, and attorneys in fact are fiduciaries.

FIDUCIARY: A person holding a position of trust. Agents, trustees, executors, administrators, and attorneys in fact are fiduciaries.

FNMA: Abbreviation for Federal National Mortgage Association ("Fannie Mae").

FORECLOSURE: Procedure whereby property pledged as security for a debt is sold to pay the debt in the event of default.

FORFEITURE: Loss of anything of value due to failure to perform.

FRAUD: An intentional false representation or concealment of a material fact which is used to induce another person to act, in which the act causes a loss of property or legal rights.

"FREE AND CLEAR": "Free" means a freehold estate, i.e., one of indefinite duration, and "clear" indicates no money encumbrances against the title.

FUNCTIONAL OBSOLESCENSE: Loss in value due to out-of-date, old-fashioned, or poorly designed equipment. A type of depreciation.

GI LOANS: A guaranteed loan available to veterans under a federal government program administered by the Veterans Administration.

GIFT DEED: A deed used to make a gift of real estate.

GRANT DEED: Customary document used in California to transfer title to real property.

GRANTEE: The purchaser; the person to whom a grant is made.

GRANTOR: The owner of the title being granted. The person who makes a grant.

GROSS INCOME: Total income before deduction of expenses or vacancy factor.

GROSS MULTIPLIER: "Rule of Thumb" method of appraising income property. Establishes the value based upon a multiple of the gross annual income.

GROUND RENT: Earnings of improved property credited to earning of the ground itself after allowance is made for earnings of improvement.

GUARANTEE OF TITLE: A guarantee by an abstract company or title company that title is vested as shown on the guarantee. Backed only the assets or reserves of the guarantor.

HIGHEST AND BEST USE: That use which is most likely to produce the greatest net return to the land and/or building over a given period of time.

HOMESTEAD: A limited exemption against certain money judgments allowed a homeowner. A home upon which the owner has recorded a declaration of homestead.

HYPOTHECATE: To make property security for a dept without giving up possession of it.

MUTUAL CONSENT: Both parties approve or assent to the terms of a contract freely.

NATURAL PERSON: A living person contrasted to a legal entity, a corporation. NEGOTIABLE INSTRUMENT: A promissory note or check which meets certain legal requirements, allowing it to circulate freely in commerce.

NET LISTING: A listing which provides that the broker may retain as his commission, that part of the sale price above a specified amount (used in mobile home sales).

NET SPENDABLE: The cash remaining from the gross income, after deducting operating expenses, principal and interest payments, and income taxes.

NOTICE OF ABANDONMENT: Document recorded to terminate a homestead.

NOTICE TO PAY RENT OR QUIT: A 3-day notice required by law before a tenant, delinquent in rental payments, may be evicted by suite.

OBSOLESCENCE: Loss in value to reduced desirability and usefulness. May be functionally or economically obsolete.

OFFSET STATEMENT: Statement of owner or lender setting forth the present status of a loan against the property. A tenant's declaration of his interest in the property.

OPEN LISTING: A listing providing that the broker is to receive a commission if he is the first person to obtain a buyer ready, willing, and able to purchase the property on the terms of the listing, or on other terms acceptable to the owner.

OPTION: A right given to a person to buy, sell, or lease property within a stated period and under certain specified terms.

OPTIONEE: The person who receives an option on property.

OPTIONOR: The owner of the title who gives the option.

ORAL CONTRACT: A verbal or spoken contract.

"OR MORE": Clause in a trust deed or note which permits an early pay-off of the loan.

OWNERSHIP AND LEGAL RIGHT OF POSSESSION: Lawful title to something.

PARTIAL RECONVEYANCE DEED: A deed used to reconvey a portion of land encumbered by a blanket mortgage of trust deed.
PARTIAL RELEASE CLAUSE: A clause in a mortgage or trust deed which provides for release of part of the property from the mortgage or trust deed upon part payment of all or part of the debt.

PARTNERSHIP: Two or more persons joined together for the operation of a business, sharing the profits in certain proportions.

PHYSICAL DETERIORATION: loss in value resulting from wear and tear.
POINTS: A point is one percent of the amount of the loan, paid to the lender at the time the loan is made in order to obtain the loan.

POLICE POWER: The right of the state to regulate those of private property for the protection of the health, safety, mortals, or general welfare of the public.

POWER OF ATTORNEY: instrument used to appoint an attorney-in-fact.

POWER OF SALE CLAUSE: A clause in a trust deed which gives the trustee the right to sell borrower's property publicly, without a court procedure, if the borrower defaults. This clause may be put into a mortgage by agreement, whereby the lender may foreclose without a court procedure.

PREPAYMENT PENALTY: A clause in a note which provides for a penalty in the event of an early pay-off of the note.

PRIMARY FINANCING: The trust deed and note that has first priority.

PRIMARY MORTGAGE MARKET: The market where loans are made directly to borrowers.

PRINCIPAL: The employer of an agent. Also means money or capital, as opposed to interest or income.

PRIVATE RESTRICTION: A restriction placed on real property by the grantor.

PROBATE: A minimum four-month period during which the Superior Court has jurisdiction over the administration of the estate of a deceased person.

PROBATE COURT: Superior Court which has authority over property of deceased persons, minors, and insane persons.

PROMISSORY NOTE: A written contract containing a promise to pay a definite amount of money at a future time.
PRORATE: To divide equally or proportionally to time or use.

PUBLIC REPORT: Report of the Real Estate Commissioner containing information about subdivided property.

PURCHASE MONEY: Deed of trust, mortgage, or land contract given to seller to secure payment of the balance of the purchase price, or a deed of trust, mortgage, or land contract on an owner-occupied dwelling of four units or less, given to a lender to secure repayment of a loan that was used to purchase property.

QUIET TITLE ACTION: A suit brought for the purpose of establishing clear title to real property or to remove a cloud on the title.

QUITCLAIM DEED: A deed used to transfer any interest in real property which the grantor may have. It contains no warranties of any kind.

REAL ESTATE EDUCATION, RESEARCH, AND RECOVERY FUND: A special state fund used to foster real estate education and to provide financial relief to persons who have suffered damages, that are uncollectible, through the fraudulent practices of a licensee.

REAL PROPERTY: Land, that which is affixed to the land, that which is incidental or appurtenant to land, and that which is immovable.

REAL PROPERTY SECURITIES DEALER: A real estate broker whose license has been endorsed, permitting him to sell real estate property securities.

REALTOR: A member of a local real estate board which is affiliated with the National Association of Real Estate Boards (NAREB).

RECORD: To file for record in the office of the Country Recorder. Gives constructive notice of the contents of the document to the world.

RECOVERY FUND: A fund held by the department of Real Estate, sustained by a portion of license fees to underwrite uncollectible court judgments against licensees on the basis of fraud, etc.

REGRESSION: An appraising principal that holds that a high valued property placed in a neighborhood of lower valued property seeks the level of the lower valued properties.

RELEASE CLAUSE: A stipulation in a trust deed or mortgage which provides that a specific described lot or area will be removed from the blanket lien upon the payment of a specific sum of money.

RENT: Consideration paid for the use and possession of a property.

REPRODUCTION COST: The cost of reproducing a new replica property on the basis of current prices with the same or closely similar materials.

REQUEST FOR NOTICE OF DEFAULT: A recorded notice made by the beneficiary of a trust deed, requesting that he be notified in the event that foreclosure proceedings are commenced by another party of interest.

RESCIND: To cancel a contract from the beginning, restoring the parties to their original positions.

RESERVATION: A right retained by a grantor in conveying property.

RESTRICTION: An encumbrance which limits the use of real estate in some way.

REVOCATION: Nullification of an offer to contract or an annulment of a license.

RIGHT OF SURVIVORSHIP: The right of a joint tenant to automatically acquire the interest of a deceased joint tenant.

SECONDARY FINANCING: Junior trust deeds or mortgages.

SECONDARY MORTGAGE MARKET: Market place for the sale and purchase of existing trust deeds and mortgages.

SEPARATE PROPERTY: Property owned by a husband or wife which is not community property.

SINKING FUND: A fund set aside from the income property which, with accrued interest, will pay for the replacement of improvements.

SOCIAL OR ECONOMIC OBSOLESCENCE: A loss in value of property due to factors outside the property.

SPECIFIC PERFORMANCE: A doctrine of contract laws by which a party is compelled by the court to perform his agreement.
SPENDABLE INCOME: The money remaining from the gross income after deducting operating expenses, principal and interest payments, and the in come tax attributable to income.

STATUTE OF FRAUDS: Law which requires certain contracts to be in writing.

STATUTE OF LIMITATIONS: The law that specifies the time limits in which legal action must be instigated to be enforceable in court.

STRAIGHT NOTE: A note in which the principal is paid in one sum.

STREET IMPROVEMENT: ACT OF 1911: Act which gives the local governing body the right to order street improvements and bill the owners for the work, or pay the costs through a bond issue and permit the owners to pay off the bond through a special assessment.

SUBDIVISION: Division of land into 5 or more parcels with the intent to sell, lease, or finance, now or any time in the future.

SUBJECT TO: Method of taking over a loan without taking on the responsibility of a deficiency judgment.

SUBORDINATION CLAUSE: A clause in a mortgage or trust deed by which the lender relinquishes his priority to a subsequent mortgage or trust deed. It benefits the borrower.

SUBSTITUTION: An appraising principal that holds that when two or more properties with substantially the same utility are available, the one with the lowest price receives the greatest demand.

TAKE-OUT LOAN: A long-term loan that replaces the interim construction loan.

TAX FREE EXCHANGE: A method of deferring capital gains by exchanging real property for other like property. Referred to as a tax shelter.

TENANCY IN COMMON: Ownership by two or more persons who told an undivided interest without right of survivorship.

TENANCY IN PARTNERSHIP: Ownership by two or more persons who unite their property in a lawful business venture.

TESTATE: Leaving a will upon death.

TITLE INSURANCE: Insurance to protect rights of beneficiary lender and trustor – good just once.

TOPOGRAPHY: Nature of the surface of land; its contour and elevation as shown by lines on a map.

TOWNSHIP: A unit of land containing 36 square miles and is six miles long on each side.

TRUST DEED (Deed of Trust): A deed by which a trustor conveys his title to the trustee as security for the payment of a debt.

TRUSTEE: One who holds legal title to property for a special purpose without being the actual (beneficial) owner. A trustee is one of the parties to every trust deed.

TRUSTEE'S DEED: Deed given by the trustee when property is sold under the power of sale in a trust deed.

TRUSTOR: Borrower in a trust deed. One who deeds his property to a trustee in a trust deed transaction.

UNDIVIDED INTEREST: The interest of co-owners in the entire property, which interest is indistinguishable.

UNLAWFUL DETAINER ACTION: Lawsuit to evict a tenant who unlawfully remains in possession of real propert

UNRUH ACT: Law which prohibits discrimination by agents or business establishments because of race, color, creed, or national origin.

USURY: Charging interest in excess of 10% per annum.

VARIANCE: Change in zoning of a single parcel.

VENDEE: Buyer of a thing being sold.

VENDOR: Owner of a thing being sold.

VERIFICATION: Sworn statement before a duly-qualified officer as to correctness of contents of an instrument.

VETERAN'S ADMINISTRATION: Federal governmental agency which administers GI (VA) loans.

VETERAN'S TAX EXEMPTION: An exemption of $1,000 on the assessed value of a veteran's property as provided by state law.

VOID: To have no force or effect. Unenforceable.

VOIDABLE: That which is capable of being made void, but is not void unless action is taken to make it so.

WARRENTY DEED: Deed which contains written warranties (guarantees) of title.

WRIT OF EXECUTION: A process of the court under which property is seized and sold.

ZONING: Governmental regulations relation to the use of land.

Index